W9-CTW-798

ILLUSTRATED
PATCHWORK
CROCHET

Contemporary Granny Squares
for Clothing and Home Decorating

BELLA SCHARF

ILLUSTRATED
PATCHWORK
CROCHET

Contemporary Granny Squares for Clothing and Home Decorating

Bella Scharf

Butterick Publishing

Illustrations by
Bella Scharf

Photography by
Bob Connolly

Book Design by
Bob Antler

Cover Design by
Susan Schwalb

Cover Photography by
Wometco Photographic Services, Inc.

Copyright © 1976 by
BUTTERICK PUBLISHING
161 Sixth Avenue
New York, New York 10013

A Division of American Can

Library of Congress Catalog Card Number 75–43282
International Standard Book Number 0–88421–052–9

Acknowledgment

I would like to thank my parents for instilling in me a love for hand-crafts and for encouraging me in my ventures; my students at Pratt Institute for contributing unusual patchwork crochet creations to my book; Malina Yarn Company for supplying yarn; and photographer Bob Connolly, who took special care to make the photography as effective and imaginative as possible.

Contents

6. The Newfangled Patchwork Crochet Techniques   131-146

7. Patchwork Crochet Projects   147-174

Introduction

Let me introduce you to an exciting craft that is bound to give you hours of enjoyment and creative challenge — patchwork crochet. You may have heard of the "granny square method" — lots of square motifs crocheted in a multitude of colors and then joined together into afghans, vests, sweaters, hats, and scarves. The craft of "patchwork crochet" is the "granny square" concept taken much further. Anything that is crocheted in small units — square, round, rectangular, or odd-shaped — and then sewn together is patchwork crochet.

In the popular craft of "fabric patchwork," pieces of fabric are cut into geometric shapes and then sewn together to form a continuous material that has a distinct pattern. This fabric could be fashioned into any number of delightful articles ranging from quilts to garments. Every fabric patchwork creation is an exercise in imaginative use of color and arrangement of geometric shapes with each design as individual as the person who created it. Though certain fabrics are more suitable for this craft, the variety of multicolored and multitextured scraps left over from other sewing projects

9

can also be joined together effectively into enchanting patchwork items. This book will show you how the charm, gaiety, and quaintness that is so appealing in fabric patchwork can be captured in crocheting.

The craft of crocheting, defined, is the forming of a fabric by looping yarn together with a hook. With patchwork crochet, you can obtain very exciting fabric textures with even the simplest stitches and color combinations. By experimenting with unusual, unconventional materials, such as metallics and ropes, you can introduce even greater interest. The excitement and challenge of working with patchwork crochet is in the creation of a variety of harmonious color combinations and textural variations for each of the basic patchwork units.

The possibility for color and yarn experimentation is one prominent aspect of patchwork crochet. Another is all the dramatic things you can construct with this fascinating craft. You can have an adventure in creativity by exploring the many two- and three-dimensional items that can be fashioned from basic geometric shapes. Afghans, shawls, and scarves are a natural for this craft. Other decorative items, hats, baby clothes, sweaters, vests, and even wallhangings can be constructed effectively from little crocheted pieces.

From a practical viewpoint, patchwork crochet offers you an opportunity to use up very small amounts of leftover yarn and even to recycle yarn pulled from sweaters you no longer wear. Use of different textures and colors in one project only enhances the beauty and patchwork quality of the item.

There are many practical reasons for getting involved in the craft. Crochet is easy to master and patchwork crochet projects are portable. Even if you are a novice in crocheting, you can learn and master the technique of constructing one motif and then keep repeating the process until you have enough units to join together into a project. After crocheting the same motif a few times the stitch pattern and the process of forming the shape will be easy to remember so there is no longer any need to keep referring back to the instructions. You can crochet another motif whenever you have a free moment—on trains, planes, and in cars, at the doctor's office, or while relaxing at home.

This book explores the variety of approaches possible in patchwork crochet. And it does so visually, with every technique not only explained, but also fully illustrated. The drawings are clear, with each stitch distinct and visible. As you work each individual patchwork unit, you can see exactly how it should look at each successive step.

Not only is the popular granny square and its variations shown, but also newer, more experimental forms of patchwork crochet, such as crocheting into fabric, leather, and wood. There is even an exciting new idea for group crochet projects—"The Patchwork Crocheting Bee"—that is reminiscent of the old-time quilting bee.

Patchwork crochet is a new approach to an age-old craft. Once you learn to do even one simple patchwork unit you can proceed to create a myriad of interesting fashions, decorative home furnishings, accessories, and gift and bazaar items.

1

The Basics of Crocheting

Very few tools and materials are needed for patchwork crochet. A crochet hook (or a selection of hooks in different sizes) and yarn are the basics. In addition, you also need a pair of scissors, a measuring tape, and a large-eyed needle to use for weaving loose ends of yarn into the work and for sewing the patchwork components together. All of these supplies can be purchased at most craft shops, variety, and department stores very inexpensively.

Crochet is not difficult to learn, but practice is necessary in order to develop the proper coordination for working with the hook and the yarn. All of the crochet stitches, including the fancy ones, are a variation of a few basic stitches. Learn and practice these stitches first. When you are adept at forming them and feel relaxed and comfortable holding the hook and the yarn, proceed to the exciting patchwork techniques featured in the book.

About Hooks

The crochet hook comes in a variety of sizes, each designed for use with a different weight of yarn. Hooks are made of either steel, aluminum, bone, plastic, or wood. The fine, steel hooks are used in working with crochet cotton and other fine yarns, the aluminum and plastic hooks are geared for wool and wool-like synthetic yarns of varied weights, and giant size plastic or wood hooks are used generally for heavy rug yarn. The following are the most popular hook sizes. In each category, as you proceed from left to right, the sizes become larger.

STEEL— 2 1 0 00
ALUMINUM— C D E F G H I J K
GIANT PLASTIC AND WOOD— Q ($\frac{5}{8}$" diameter)   S ($\frac{3}{4}$" diameter)

About Yarns

For patchwork crochet a variety of yarns can be used. The most popular kind, and the one used for most of the items featured in this book, is a 4-ply worsted-weight knitting yarn which is made of either 100% wool or synthetic fiber, such as acrylic. Worsted-weight yarn is generally compatible with either size G, H, I, or J hook. Available in a great variety of colors, it can be used for afghans, bedspreads, and other home decorating items, as well as most garments and accessories. Other yarn possibilities are:

Crochet Cotton: Available in a few weights, this fine cotton yarn is non-stretchy and is used for tablecloths, doilies, as well as fine garments. Use steel hooks 6 through 00.

Cotton String: A package-wrapping yarn, sometimes called butcher twine, is available in hardware stores. Use hooks G, H, I.

Fingering or Baby Yarn: A fine, soft, 100% wool or synthetic fiber yarn, is appropriate for baby items. Use hooks C, D, E.

Sport Yarn: A 3-ply wool or synthetic yarn which is soft, stretchy, and a finer worsted-weight yarn. Use hooks E, F, G.

Rug Yarn or Bulky Yarn: A 3-ply heavy-weight yarn, available in wool, cotton, or acrylic and is used for rugs and bulky garments. Use hooks J, K, Q.

Mohair: A fuzzy, soft medium-thin wool yarn used for garments, accessories, and afghans. Use hooks G, H, I, J.

Metallic Yarn: Rather thin yarn with a metallic texture of either silver, gold, or colored metallic effects used for jewelry and eveningwear. Use hooks E, F, G, H.

Multi-Colored or Ombre Yarn: Either sport or worsted-weight, this yarn has a dyed multi-color effect with a color change every few inches. Use hooks E through J.

Rattail: A yarn consisting of rayon wrapped around a cotton core usually used for macrame, it achieves interesting effects in crochet. Use hooks I, J, K.

Jute: A rope-like yarn, made of jute, which comes in a variety of colors, and is appropriate for decorative accessories, such as rugs, placemats, planters. Use hooks J, K.

Raffia or Synthetic Straw: A natural or synthetic straw, is appropriate for placemats, lampshades, planters, bags. Use hooks G, H, I.

Crepe Yarn: A non-stretchy rayon-blend yarn with texture and sheen used for fashion items. Use hooks E, F, G.

NEW YARN IDEAS: If you choose to experiment with unusual materials in your patchwork crochet project, there are many exciting possibilities to consider. Knitted and woven fabric, when cut into thin strips, can be crocheted quite easily provided you use an appropriately large hook. So can strips cut from worn-out nylon hosiery. Consider, too, such non-yarn type materials as very thin and pliable copper wire, thin strips of plastic wrap, and paper cord that is used to wrap packages. Some of these unusual ideas are explained in more detail in Chapter 6: The Newfangled Patchwork Crochet Techniques, page 131.

Crochet Language and How to Read It

Since most crochet stitches have lengthy names, crochet directions are written in a shorthand language. The shorthand is an abbreviation of the stitch name. The following are the standard crochet abbreviations and their meanings. As you work the various patchwork techniques in this book, refer back to this page until you are familiar with all the abbreviations.

sp(s)	space(s)
ch	chain
ch st	chain stitch
sl st	slip stitch
sc	single crochet
st	stitch
sts	stitches
hdc	half double crochet
dc	double crochet
trc	triple crochet
dtrc	double triple crochet
yo	yarn over (hook)
sk	skip
beg	beginning
dec	decrease
inc	increase
tog	together

In addition to abbreviations of stitch names, crochet language includes the following symbols:

Asterisk: The asterisk (*) serves as a marker in a row or round of stitches. When you are told to "repeat from * 4 times," for example, you work the specified stitches the first time. Then you return to the * and repeat what is written after it four times.

Parentheses: One function of parentheses is to enclose a number of stitches which must all be worked into one space or stitch.

example: (3 dc, ch 3, 3 dc) in corner ch-3 sp

That means that you must work three double crochet stitches, chain 3, and three more double crochet stitches into the chain 3 space at the corner of a square. Other times parentheses enclose instructions for stitches to be done several times.

example: (dc, ch 2) 11 times into ring.

That means that you must work a double crochet stitch followed by a chain-2 eleven times into the ring. In other words, do what is in the parentheses the specified number of times.

GAUGE:

When constructing a patchwork crochet item to a specific size or fit, it is essential to first know the gauge of the component To arrive at the gauge, or measurements, of a motif, simply measure it (Figure 1). If the motif is too small, work it again with a larger hook. If it is too large, try working with a smaller hook.

To obtain the gauge of crochet rows, first measure horizontally to determine how many stitches there are in a one-inch or two-inch space. Then measure it vertically to find how many rows measure one or two inches. (Figure 2)

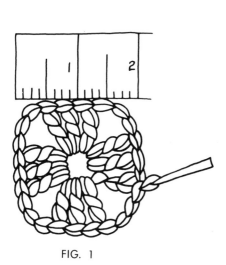

FIG. 1

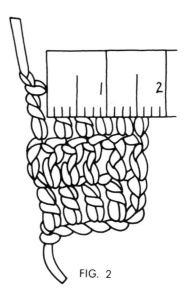

FIG. 2

Record this information and be sure that all motifs for that project are crocheted to that gauge so that the pieces will fit together.

Basic Knots, Chains, and Stitches

THE SLIP KNOT

All crocheting begins with the slip knot. It is the first loop you place on the hook. Once the slip knot is in place, you chain a group of stitches which will become the foundation for your crochet pattern.

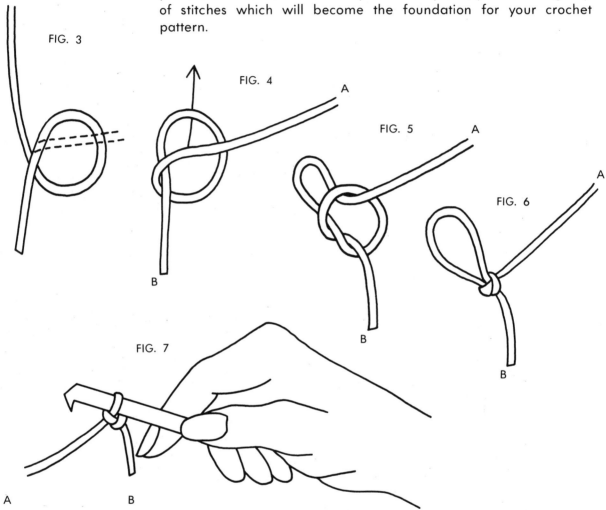

FIG. 3

FIG. 4

FIG. 5

FIG. 6

FIG. 7

Working on a flat surface, hold cut end of yarn B and form it into a circle (Figure 3). Place end A across the circle, cutting circle in half (Figure 4). Pull center strand up through circle with one hand, while grasping ends A and B with the other hand (Figure 5). A knot will form (Figure 6).

Insert hook into loop and pull end A so that loop becomes smaller and conforms to the size of the hook. Hook should be held as you would hold a dinner knife (Figure 7).

HOLDING HOOK AND YARN

Grasp end B with thumb and index finger of left hand, while raising left forefinger. Yarn is draped over forefinger, while pinky and ring fingers are folded over towards palm. These two fingers serve as a tension spool, as on a sewing machine. By resting against the yarn loosely, they perpetually loosen and tighten their hold on the yarn as it passes through the left hand. Allowing the yarn a proper, even tension is a skill that must be developed through practice. The tighter the hold of these two fingers on the yarn, the smaller and tighter the stitches. The tightness or looseness of the stitches also depends on the weight of the yarn, the hook size, and even your degree of relaxation when you crochet.

THE CHAIN (ch)

Make a slip knot. To begin chaining, pass hook *under* the yarn and catch it with the hook. Pull the yarn back through the loop on the hook. What is formed is a first chain (ch). Passing the hook

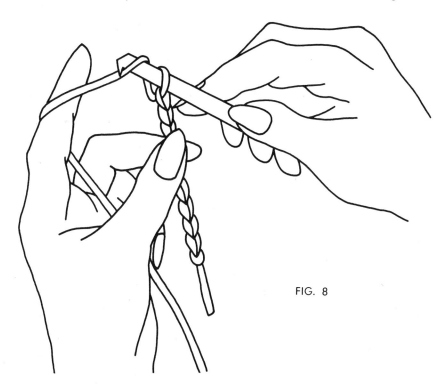

FIG. 8

under the yarn is called yarn over (yo). Repeat this chaining process of yarn over and pulling loop through last chain as many times as the number of chains you require (Figure 8). The knot *does not* count as a chain.

As you complete four or five chains, move the thumb and index finger further up the chain towards the hook for better control of the work. Be sure the chaining row remains even and symmetrical, with a series of V's, one coming out of the other.

THE SLIP STITCH (sl st)

The slip stitch is used mainly to join rounds of crocheting together. It has no height and cannot be worked in rows or rounds as all the other stitches.

Insert hook in chain, yarn over, and pull a loop through the chain (Figure 9). Pull new loop through old loop on hook.

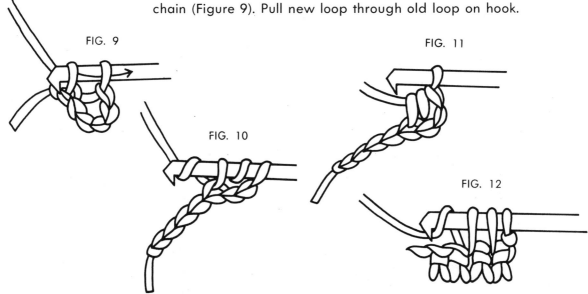

FIG. 9

FIG. 10

FIG. 11

FIG. 12

THE SINGLE CROCHET STITCH (sc)

To practice, begin with a chain of 15 stitches. Insert hook in second chain from hook, yarn over, and pull a loop through the chain (Figure 10). Yarn over again and pull new loop through two loops on hook (Figure 11). Work a single crochet stitch in every chain across. At end of row, chain 1 (Figure 12). Turn piece.

Row 2: Single crochet in every sc stitch across. Chain 1, turn. Repeat Row 2 for consecutive rows of single crochet.

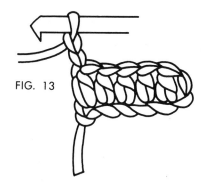

FIG. 13

To Increase 1 SC ST: Work 2 single crochet stitches in one stitch.

To Decrease 1 SC ST: Pull a loop through first stitch. Then, pull a loop through next stitch. Yarn over and pull yarn through all three loops on hook (Figure 13).

THE HALF DOUBLE CROCHET STITCH (hdc)

To practice, begin with a chain of 15 stitches. Yarn over hook once (Figure 14). Insert hook in third chain from hook, yarn over, and pull a loop through chain (Figure 15). Yarn over and pull yarn through all three loops on hook (Figure 16). Work a half double crochet stitch in next chain and every chain across. Chain 2 (Figure 17). Turn.

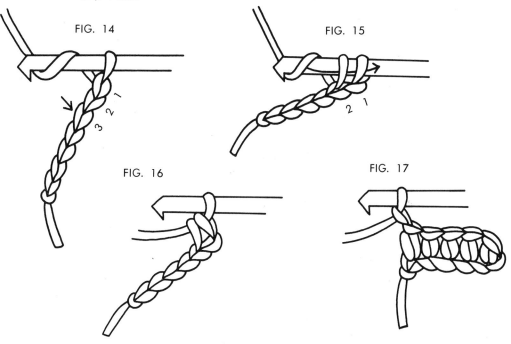

FIG. 14

FIG. 15

FIG. 16

FIG. 17

Row 2: Half double crochet in first stitch and every stitch across. Chain 2, turn.

Repeat Row 2 for consecutive rows.

THE DOUBLE CROCHET STITCH (dc)

To practice, begin with a chain of 15 stitches. Yarn over hook once (Figure 18). Insert hook in fourth chain from hook, yarn over, and pull a loop through the chain (Figure 19). Yarn over and pull yarn through two loops on hook (Figure 20). Yarn over and pull yarn through last two loops on hook (Figure 21). Work a double crochet stitch in next chain and every chain across. Chain 2 (Figure 22). Turn.

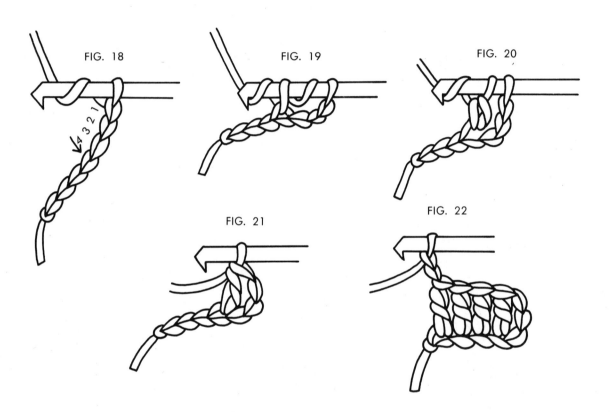

FIG. 18   FIG. 19   FIG. 20

FIG. 21   FIG. 22

Row 2: Double crochet in top of first stitch, picking up both loops of stitch; double crochet in every stitch across. Work double crochet in third chain of the chain-3 at end of row (Figure 23). Chain 2, turn. (The chain-3 counts as one double crochet stitch.)

Row 3: Double crochet in every stitch across. Chain 2, turn (Figure 24).

Repeat Row 3 for consecutive rows of double crochet stitch.

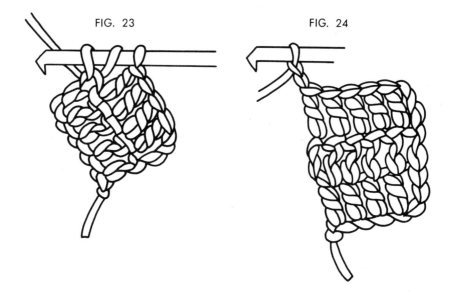

FIG. 23   FIG. 24

To Increase 1 DC ST: Work 2 double crochet stitches in one stitch (Figure 25).

To Decrease 1 DC ST: Yarn over, pull a loop through first stitch, yarn over, and pull yarn through 2 loops on hook; yarn over and pull a loop through next stitch, yarn over, and pull through 2 loops on hook. Yarn over and pull through all 3 loops on hook. (Figure 26).

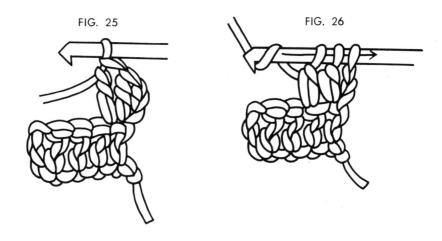

FIG. 25   FIG. 26

THE TRIPLE CROCHET STITCH (trc)

To practice, begin with a chain of 15 stitches. Yarn over hook twice (Figure 27). Insert hook in fifth chain from hook, yarn over, and pull a loop through chain, *yarn over and pull yarn through two loops on hook; repeat from * 2 more times (Figure 28). Work a triple crochet stitch in next chain and every chain across. Chain 3 to turn.

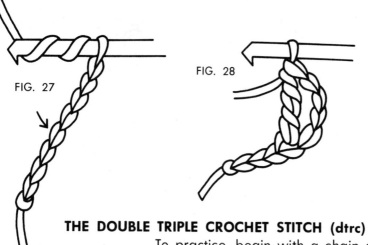

FIG. 27

FIG. 28

THE DOUBLE TRIPLE CROCHET STITCH (dtrc)

To practice, begin with a chain of 15 stitches. Yarn over hook three times (Figure 29). Insert hook in sixth chain from hook and pull a loop through chain, *yarn over and pull yarn through two loops on hook; repeat from * 3 more times (Figure 30). Work a double triple crochet stitch in next chain and every chain across. Chain 3 to turn.

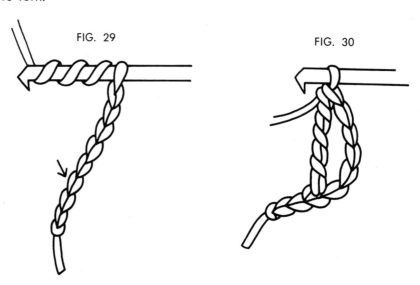

FIG. 29

FIG. 30

Patchwork Crochet Techniques

This book features a variety of patchwork crochet components. They are alternately referred to as units, pieces, or motifs. There are triangles, squares, hexagons, circles, octagons, and strips. Some are lacy, some solid in texture. Some are effective when done in a variety of colors. Some look best in one color.

What most of the components have in common, though, is that they are usually worked from the center out, rather than in rows as in other crochet techniques. The first circular series of stitches, called "round" of stitches, is usually worked into a circle of chain stitches. To understand this concept, imagine working into a plastic ring (Figure 31). Likewise, you can form a ring out of yarn by crocheting a number of chains and joining them together into a ring. The number of chains you crochet to form the ring will depend on what is specified in the instructions, but the number is usually no less than four or five chains (Figure 32). Insert hook into the first chain made (after the knot), yarn over, and pull yarn through the chain (Figure 33). Pull the new loop through the original loop on the hook, completing a slip stitch. What results is a ring into which to work the first round of stitches. When working the stitches into the ring, insert the hook into the center hole, or space, and crochet *around* the edge of the ring (Figure 34). Do not work the stitches into the individual chains which form the ring.

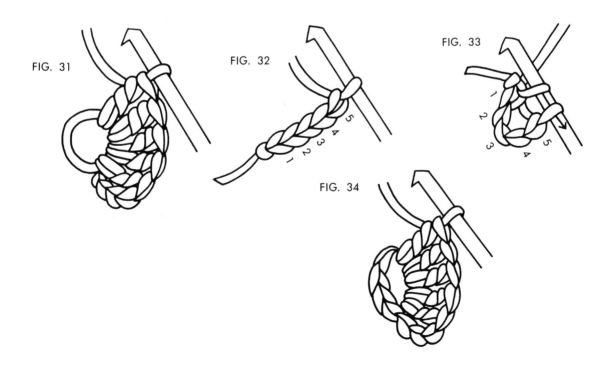

FIG. 31

FIG. 32

FIG. 33

FIG. 34

BEGINNING A ROUND

In most of the motifs, you are asked to chain a few more stitches before working into the ring (Figure 35). These few chains serve to bring the hook up to the height of the stitches that will be made into the ring. Though they do not resemble a stitch, these chains are considered to be the *very first stitch* of the round. For example, if the first round worked into the ring consists of 12 double crochet stitches, there will be 11 double crochet stitches and a chain-3 (Figure 36).

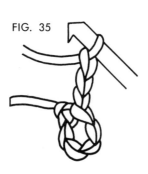

FIG. 35

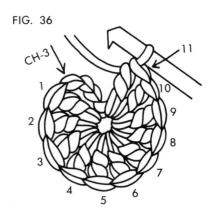

FIG. 36

NOTE: It is important to remember that as you work the stitches into the ring, you must continuously move them to the right (if you are right-handed), sliding them along the ring. This is to allow all the necessary stitches to fit into the ring.

ENDING A ROUND

When all stitches of a round are made, the first and last stitches of the round are joined with a slip stitch. Insert hook into the third (top) chain of the initial chain-3, pull through a loop (Figure 37), pull the new loop through the loop on the hook, thereby making a slip stitch.

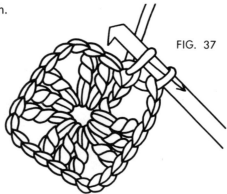

FIG. 37

FASTENING OFF

Fastening off is done at the end of a round when the next round is to be made with a different color yarn or at the end of a motif if it is made of one color yarn. After working the slip stitch to join the round, chain 1. Cut yarn, leaving at least a 3 inch end (Figure 38). Enlarge loop by pulling hook away from work until cut end comes through the chain-1 loop. Pull cut end to tighten the chain-1 into a knot (Figure 39).

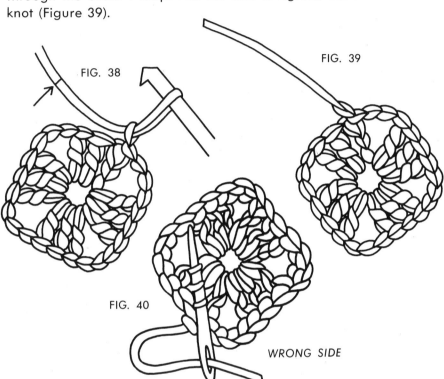

FIG. 38

FIG. 39

FIG. 40

WRONG SIDE

WEAVING ENDS THROUGH BACK OF WORK

All cut ends of yarn hanging from a motif must be woven into the wrong side of the unit so that the piece will have a neat, clean look. Thread cut end of yarn into a tapestry needle. On back of work, run needle through the top loops of two or three stitches once (Figure 40), then again through other stitches in the opposite direction. Cut leftover end close to work. Back of work will look as neat as the right side. This weaving in must be done with all yarn ends. It can be done at the end of every round or when all the rounds of a motif have been completed.

CHANGING COLORS

Changing Colors in the Middle of a Row or a Round: In Color A, yarn over and pull a loop through next chain or stitch, yarn over and pull yarn through 2 loops on hook; cut Color A. Pull Color B through remaining 2 loops on hook (Figure 41).

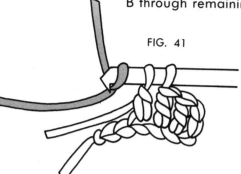

FIG. 41

Attaching New Color Yarn: Most patchwork motifs require a color change on every round. The instructions indicate exactly where the new color yarn is to be attached. There are many methods of attaching yarn to a crocheted piece. The two methods featured here are both simple to do. Try them both and use whichever method suits you best.

Method 1: Insert end of new color yarn through space where second round is to begin. (If new color should be attached in a stitch, use a crochet hook or thread the end into a tapestry needle

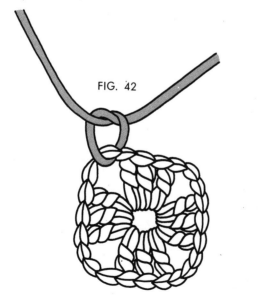

FIG. 42

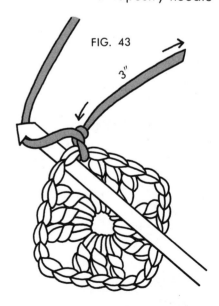

FIG. 43

3"

and use it to pull the end through.) Make a simple knot, tying the two ends together (Figure 42). Tighten knot, leaving a 3 inch end, and have knot fall at far right corner of space. Insert hook into space and pull through a loop (Figure 43). Proceed with working the next round.

Method 2: Make a slip knot in the new color, leaving a 3 inch end. Insert hook into loop, then insert hook into specified space or stitch and pull through another loop (Figure 44). Work a slip stitch, pulling new loop through original loop on hook. Proceed with working next round.

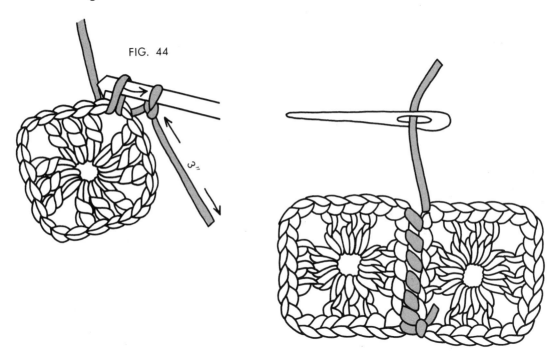

FIG. 44

SEWING COMPLETED MOTIFS TOGETHER

Sewing patchwork components together is the most effective, flattest method of attaching them. To do this, simply place one motif on top of another, right sides together. Thread tapestry needle with matching color yarn. Attach yarn at one corner of one motif, fastening it securely by stitching through corner stitches twice. Then overcast the edge stitches of both motifs together, picking up only one thread from each stitch on each motif's edge. Work to other corner (Figure 45). Secure yarn again by stitching into edge stitches two or three times. Cut yarn close to work.

CROCHETING COMPLETED MOTIFS TOGETHER

If desired, motifs could be loosely slip-stitched or single-crocheted together instead of sewn. For this method, you also place the motifs one on top of another, right sides together. Attach the yarn at one corner through corner stitches of both motifs using one of the methods for attaching a new color yarn. Then single crochet or *loosely* slip stitch through both motifs, crocheting matching edge stitches of both motifs together. Fasten off at next corner. Then weave the cut ends that remain on either side of the seam into the back of the work.

You could also consider overlapping the two motifs, but having their wrong sides facing each other, and do the crocheting on the right side of the work. That would give a ridged effect to the seam and, when done in a contrasting color yarn, could serve as a trim between the motifs.

FINISHING TECHNIQUES

In patchwork crochet, you can be creative from the start to the finish of your project. Not only are your choices of patchwork techniques numerous, but you have a variety of finishing techniques to choose from. Edgings and fringes serve as adornments on a patchwork crochet item. They add that final touch, the accent which many projects require to complete their handcrafted look. Sometimes a new color is introduced in the edging to spice up a piece. Usually edgings are worked in a color that appears in the patchwork units, a neutral color that blends with all the other shades.

Most decorative items for the home, such as afghans, bedspreads, and wallhangings, become more extravagant and voluminous when they are bordered with fringe around all the edges. Shawls also need the added fullness of crocheted or yarn fringe on the bottom edges for a dramatic, drapey effect. A picot or shell edging makes a lovely, subtle trim on a garment—around the neckline, armholes, sleeve edges, and hem.

SINGLE CROCHET EDGING When all patchwork crochet components are sewn together into an afghan, garment, or accessory, the borders of the piece are usually edged with one, two, or even three rounds of single crochet. To do this, attach a matching or contrasting color yarn in any stitch on any side of the piece. Work a single crochet in same stitch, then single crochet along the edge till the corner. Work a single crochet in *every* stitch or *every other* stitch along the edge, distributing stitches evenly for a flat edge.

Make sure that the edging is neither too loose (too many stitches) nor too tight (too few stitches).

In the corner stitch or space, work three single crochet stitches (Figure 46). Continue working the other sides and corners of the piece the same way. At the end of the round, slip stitch into the first single crochet stitch made.

To Make a Second Round: Ch 1, *sc in next st and every st till middle sc of the 3-sc group at corner, 3 sc in corner st; repeat from * around. Sl st in first sc made. Repeat this last round for consecutive rounds.

NOTE: Before doing any one of the following novelty edgings on an item, you must do at least one or two rounds of single crochet on the edge.

FRINGE EDGING Wind yarn around a cardboard gauge, which, when folded, is the desired size of the completed fringe, say 6 inches. Cut ends at one side (Figure 47). Fold three or four strands in half. Insert hook in stitch and pull the fold through the stitch (Figure 48). Pull the six strands completely through the fold (Figure 49). Pull the six strands away from the edge to tighten the knot. Skip the next stitch or two and insert fringe in the next stitch.

FIG. 46

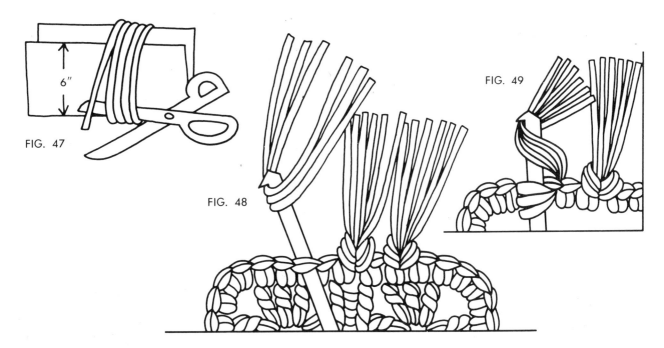

FIG. 47

FIG. 48

FIG. 49

SHELL EDGING Attach yarn in any sc st, *skip 2 sts, 7 dc in next st, skip 2 sts, sc in next st (Figure 50); repeat from *around, working a shell into each corner st also.

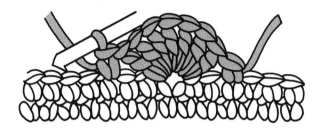

PICOT EDGING Attach yarn in any sc st, *ch 3, sc in third ch from hook (Figure 51), sl st in next 2 sc on edge; repeat from * around (Figure 52).

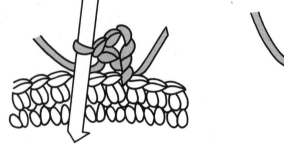
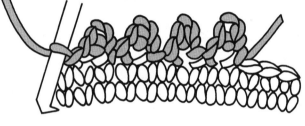

CROCHETED BALL FRINGE Attach yarn in any sc st, *ch desired amount (about 8–9 chs), work 7 sc in second ch from hook (Figure 53). Sl st in first sc made to form ball (Figure 54). Sl st in every remaining ch till edge, sl st in next 2 sc on edge (Figure 55); repeat from * around. For novelty, try chaining a different amount for each ball fringe.

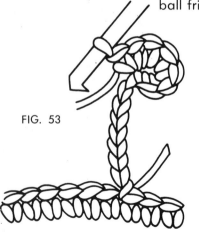

FIG. 53

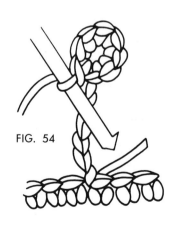

FIG. 54

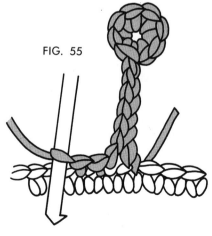

FIG. 55

COLOR PLATE **1**

1. Rattail 2. Jute 3. Fabric Strips 4. Mohair Yarn 5. Chenille Yarn 6. Synthethic Straw 7. Cotton String 8. Metallic Yarn 9. Multi-Colored Yarn 10. Rug Yarn 11. Crepe Yarn 12. Crochet Cotton

COLOR PLATE **2**   DRAPED ON CHAIR: *Afghan*. Hexagon Granny Three, page 72. TOP CENTER:
Pillow. Mixed-media crochet with suede, page 137. CENTER RIGHT: *Pillow*.
Strip One, page 117. BOTTOM LEFT: *Planter*, page 160. Strip Six, page 129.
BOTTOM: *Area Rug*. Graphic Granny Four, page 104, and strips crocheted in a
stripe pattern. Rug and planter made of Malina's Acrilan Rug Yarn.

COLOR PLATE **3**

TOP: *Wall Hanging.* Graphic Granny Seven, page 110. LEFT: *Baby Afghan.* Graphic Granny Six, page 108. RIGHT: *Children's Afghan.* Graphic Granny Eight, page 112. All items made of Fruit-of-the-Loom Yarn

COLOR PLATE **4**   *Full-size-Bedspread. Granny Square Nine, page 61. Created by Sunny Lee.
Made of Malina's 100% Acrilan Yarn*

COLOR PLATE **5**   TOP: *Shawl.* Granny Square Three, page 49. CENTER AND LOWER LEFT: *Rectangular and Round Pillows.* Graphic Granny Five, page 106. LOWER CENTER: *Shawl.* Granny Square Eleven, page 65. LOWER RIGHT: *Pillow.* Granny Square Ten, page 63. All items made of Fruit-of-the-Loom Yarn.

COLOR PLATE **6**   UPPER LEFT: *Afghan.* Granny Square Three, page 49. TOP CENTER: *Afghan.*
Strip Two, page 119. CENTER: *Pillow.* Hexagon Granny Two, page 70. BOTTOM:
Afghan. Granny Square One, page 45. All items made of Malina's 100%
Acrilan Yarn

COLOR PLATE **7**

TOP: *Afghan*. Strip Five, page 126. DRAPED ON CHAIR: *Baby Afghan*. Circular Granny Two, page 77. CENTER: *Pillow*. Graphic Grannies Two and Three, page 102 and 103. RIGHT: *Pillow*. Calico Crochet Patterns One and Two, page 133 and 135. All items made of Fruit-of-the-Loom Yarn.

COLOR PLATE **8** *CRAZY QUILT.* Wall hanging, executed in the free form patchwork crochet technique, with each motif done by a different person. Piece was created in a Crocheting Bee held in author's Experimental Crafts class at Pratt Institute, Brooklyn, N.Y.

MACARONI FRINGE Attach yarn in any sc st, *ch desired amount, work 3 sc in second ch from hook, then work 3 sc in every remaining ch till edge (Figure 56). Piece will curl. Sc in next 2 sc on edge; repeat from *around.

FIG. 56

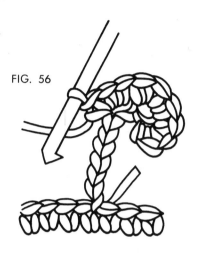

Shell Edging

Picot Edging

Ball Fringe

Macaroni Fringe

BLOCKING A FINISHED PROJECT

When a project has been completed with all patchwork components sewn together, it should be smoothed and flattened with a light steam pressing. Any discrepancy in the size of the motifs, or an undesirable puffiness of the surface, can usually be corrected by blocking.

Place the item on an ironing board and form it to the shape and the dimensions it requires in order to fit. If it is a large item, work on one area of it at a time. Saturate a paper towel or a press cloth with water, wring it out, and place it flatly on the item. Lightly place a hot iron on top of the paper towel. A hissing sound will result. Make sure the iron does not rest its weight directly on top of the crocheting. Such heavy pressing will result in a very flat texture, permanently spoiling the attractive surface. Let the steamed area dry. Then repeat the process on other areas of the project. Care should be taken not to stretch the piece out of shape in steaming it. Blocking should be done in graduated steps. If the piece is not sufficiently smooth and fabriclike after a first light pressing, repeat the procedure by pressing it again until you are satisfied with the results.

2

A Medley of Granny Squares

For many centuries people have enjoyed crocheting clever little geometric shapes and attaching them together into all sorts of articles. It is impossible to know who first thought of crocheting in the round, rather than in rows, to form these units. What is known is that during the height of popularity of crocheted lace during and after the Renaissance, various lace designs included raised floral patterns that were crocheted individually and then joined together. Over the years, separate crocheted pieces have been referred to as medallions, rosettes, and counterpanes. They have been used to make not only lace, which was usually applied as decorative insertion in garments, but also doilies, tablecloths, afghans, bedspreads, and shawls.

In pioneering days in America, a simpler version of the intricate rosette pattern emerged. It assumed a charming, quaint name—

the Granny Square—evoking the image of dedicated pioneer women working on their labors of love by candlelight. Since the granny square looked most effective when every round was done with a different color yarn, it could be crocheted in a variety of colors using those precious bits and pieces of leftover yarn which these women held so dear. Having survived through the years, the granny square is just as popular today.

This well-known patchwork crochet pattern that we all know and love initiates the following collection of geometric patchwork crochet components. The granny square is a simple, clever arrangement of groups of double crochet stitches and chain-stitch spacings which form a square. All the other seventeen motifs, whether square, hexagonal, circular, or triangular in shape, are just as simple in concept and just as easy to do. They are all worked from the center out and are formed with a series of rounds. Each consists of one or two basic stitches, but may feature a novelty stitch, such as the puff, popcorn, or cluster stitch for varied texture and interest.

Before attempting to do any of these interesting variations, first practice crocheting Granny Square One. Experiment with changing colors on every round because the essential feature of these motifs is the use of many colors.

Of all patchwork crochet techniques in this book, the units in this chapter will offer the most opportunity for color experimentation. Try making the motifs with different size hooks and the same yarn. Usually the motifs should be soft and pliable, rather than stiff and hard. Stiff, hard squares are caused by crocheting tightly with a small hook. However, the effect you choose will depend on the item you are making.

The granny square and all of its variations can be made into an assortment of articles—afghans, purses, bags, hats, sweaters, decorative household items, and wallhangings—and many others. There is no limit to the kind of yarns you can utilize. Color Plate I illustrates how the basic granny square assumes a unique look with each different yarn used.

Granny Square One *(See Afghan, Color Plate 6)*

NOTE: This Basic Granny Square is presented in unabbreviated crochet language. Instructions for all the other motifs in this book appear in crochet shorthand.

Round 1: In Color A, chain 5 (Figure 1). Slip stitch in first chain to form ring (Figure 2). Chain 3 (Figure 3). Into the ring make 2 double crochet stitches (Figure 4). Chain 3 (Figure 5). *Make 3 double crochet stitches in ring, chain 3; repeat from * 2 times. Slip stitch into the third chain of the chain-3 (Figure 6). Fasten off.

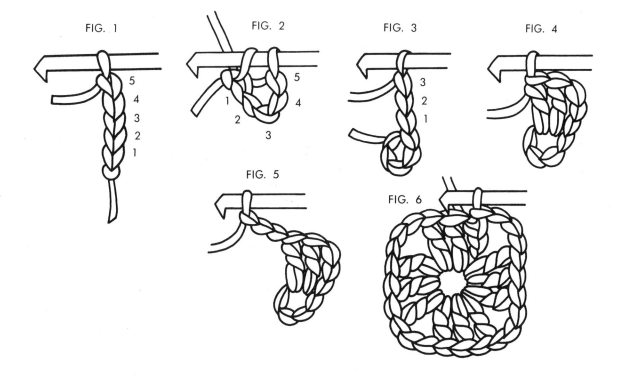

FIG. 1

FIG. 2

FIG. 3

FIG. 4

FIG. 5

FIG. 6

Round 2: Attach Color B in any chain-3 corner space (Figure 7). Chain 3. In same space, make (2 double crochet, chain 3, 3 double crochet), *chain 1, in next chain-3 corner space make (3 double crochet, chain 3, 3 double crochet) (Figure 8); repeat from * 2 more times. Chain 1, slip stitch into third chain of chain-3. Fasten off.

Round 3: Attach Color C in any chain-3 corner space, chain 3, in same space make (2 double crochet, chain 3, 3 double crochet), *chain 1, 3 double crochet in next chain-1 space, chain 1, (3 double crochet, chain 3, 3 double crochet) in next chain-3 corner space; repeat from * 2 more times (Figure 9). Chain 1, 3 double crochet in last chain-1 space, ch 1, slip stitch into third chain of chain-3. Fasten off.

FIG. 7

FIG. 8

FIG. 9

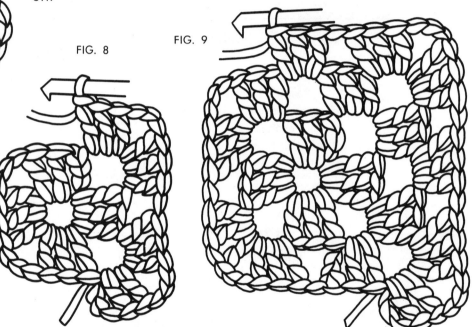

Round 4: Attach Color D in any chain-3 corner space, chain 3, in same space make (2 double crochet, chain 3, 3 double crochet), *(chain 1, 3 double crochet) in every chain-1 space to next corner, chain 1, (3 double crochet, chain 3, 3 double crochet) in next chain-3 corner space; repeat from * 2 more times. (Chain 1, 3 double crochet) in every remaining chain-1 space, chain 1, slip stitch into third chain of chain-3. Fasten off.

Repeat Round 4 for consecutive rounds.

HALF-SQUARE
To be used for shaping garments.

Row 1: In Color A, ch 5; in fifth ch from hook work 3 dc, ch 3, 3 dc, ch 1, 1 dc. Fasten off. (Figure 10)

FIG. 10

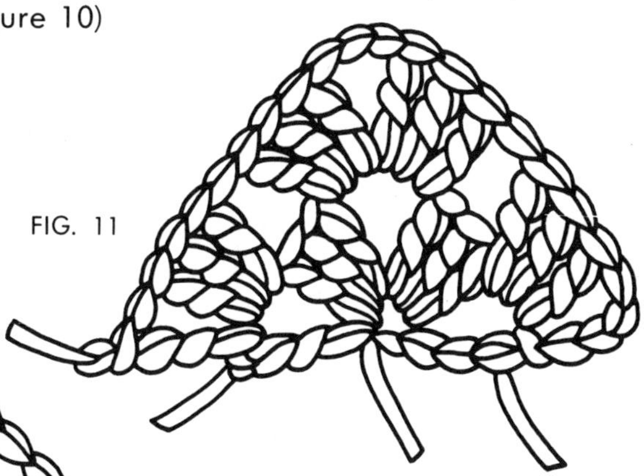

FIG. 11

FIG. 12

Row 2: Attach Color B in ch-4 sp, ch 4, 3 dc in same sp, ch 1, (3 dc, ch 3, 3 dc) in next ch-1 sp, ch 1, (3 dc, ch 1, 1 dc) in last sp. Fasten off. (Figure 11)

Row 3: Attach Color C in ch-4 sp, ch 4, 3 dc in same sp, ch 1, 3 dc in next ch-1 sp, ch 1, (3 dc, ch 3, 3 dc) in ch-3 corner sp, ch 1, 3 dc in next ch-1 sp, ch 1, (3 dc, ch 1, 1 dc) in last sp. Fasten off. (Figure 12)

Row 4: Attach Color D in ch-4 sp, 3 dc in same sp, (ch 1, 3 dc) in every ch-1 sp to corner, ch 1, (3 dc, ch 3, 3 dc) in ch-3 corner sp, (ch 1, 3 dc) in every ch-1 sp, ch 1, (3 dc, ch 1, 1 dc) in last sp. Fasten off.

Repeat Row 4 for consecutive rows.

Granny Square Two

Round 1: Ch 5, sl st in first ch to form ring, ch 3, 2 dc in ring, *ch 2, 3 dc in ring; repeat from * 2 more times, ch 2, sl st in third ch of ch-3. (Figure 1)

Round 2: Ch 3, dc in each of next 2 dc, *(2 dc, ch 2, 2 dc) in corner ch-2 space, dc in each of next 3 dc (Figure 2); repeat from * 2 more times, (2 dc, ch 2, 2 dc) in last ch-2 corner space. Sl st to third ch of ch-3.

Round 3: Ch 3, dc in each of next 4 dc, *(2 dc, ch 2, 2 dc) in ch-2 corner space, dc in each of next 7 dc (Figure 3); repeat from * 2 more times, (2 dc, ch 2, 2 dc) in last ch-2 corner space, dc in next 2 dc, sl st to third ch of ch-3. Fasten off.

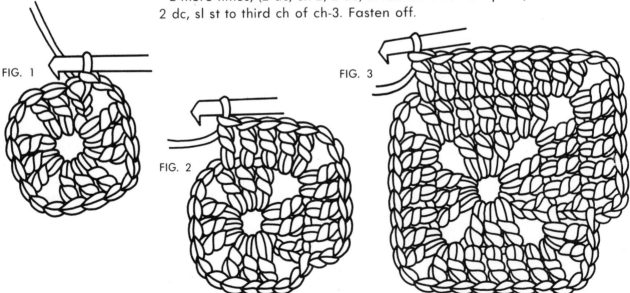

FIG. 1

FIG. 2

FIG. 3

Granny Square Three *(See Shawl, Color Plate 5 and Afghan, Color Plate 6)*

Round 1: In Color A, ch 10, sl st in first ch to form ring, (ch 10, sc into ring) 12 times (Figure 1). Fasten off. (Figure 2)

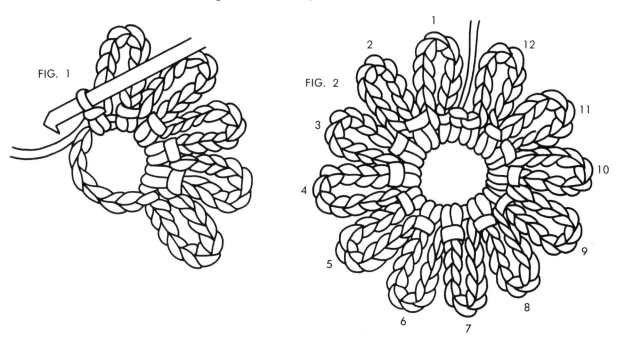

FIG. 1

FIG. 2

Round 2: Attach Color B in any ch-10 loop, ch 3, (2 dc, ch 2, 3 dc) in same loop, *3 hdc in each of next 2 loops, (3 dc, ch 2,

3 dc) in next loop; repeat from * twice more. Work 3 hdc in each of last 2 loops, sl st in third ch of ch-3. Fasten off. (Figure 3)

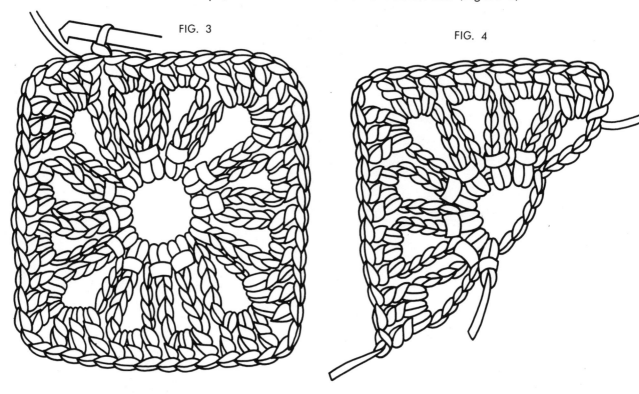

FIG. 3   FIG. 4

HALF-SQUARE
To be used for shaping garments.

Row 1: In Color A, ch 10, sl st in first ch to form ring, (ch 10, sc into ring) 7 times. Fasten off.

Row 2: Attach Color B in first loop made, ch 3, 2 dc in same loop, 3 hdc in each of next 2 loops, (3 dc, ch 2, 3 dc) in fourth loop, 3 hdc in each of next 2 loops, 3 dc in last loop. Fasten off. (Figure 4)

Granny Square Four

Round 1: In Color A, ch 6, sl st in first ch to form ring, ch 1, 8 sc into ring. Sl st in first sc made. (Figure 1)

Round 2: Pull up loop on hook to 3/4″ (Figure 2), (yo, pull up loop in first sc to 3/4″) 4 times (Figure 3), yo and through all 9 loops on hook, ch 1 tightly to fasten st (a puff st made), ch 4 (Figure 4), *(yo, pull up loop in next sc to 3/4″) 4 times, yo and through all 9 loops on hook, ch 1 tightly, ch 2, make puff st same way in next sc, ch 4; repeat from * 2 more times, make puff st in last sc, ch 2. Sl st to top of first puff st (Figure 5). Fasten off.

FIG. 1

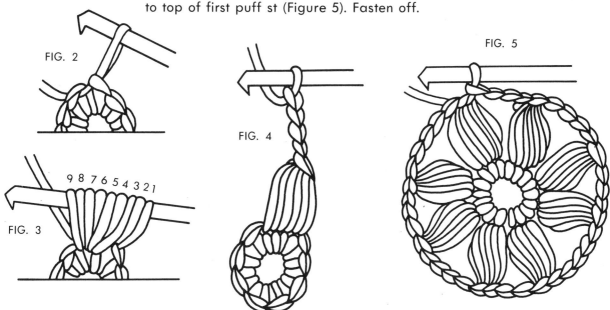

FIG. 2

FIG. 4

FIG. 5

9 8 7 6 5 4 3 2 1

FIG. 3

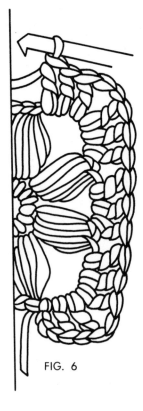

Round 3: Attach Color B in any ch-4 corner sp, ch 3, (2 dc, ch 2, 3 dc) in same sp, *3 dc in next sp, (3 dc, ch 2, 3 dc) in next corner ch-4 sp (Figure 6); repeat from * 2 times, 3 dc in last sp. Sl st to third ch of ch-3. Fasten off.

HALF-SQUARE
To be used for shaping garments.

Row 1: In Color A, ch 6, sl st in first ch to form ring, ch 1, 6 sc in ring. Fasten off. (Figure 7)

Row 2: Attach Color A in first sc made into ring, pull up loop on hook to ¾″, (yo, pull up ¾″ loop in same st) 4 times, yo and through all 9 loops on hook, ch 1 tightly, ch 2, puff st in second sc, ch 2, puff st in third sc, ch 4, puff st in fourth sc, ch 2, puff st in fifth sc, ch 2, puff st in sixth sc. Fasten off. (Figure 8)

Row 3: Attach Color B in first ch-2 sp, ch 4, 3 dc in same sp, 3 dc in next ch-2 sp, (3 dc, ch 2, 3 dc) in ch-4 sp, 3 dc in each of next two ch-2 sps, ch 1, dc once again in last sp. Fasten off. (Figure 9)

FIG. 6

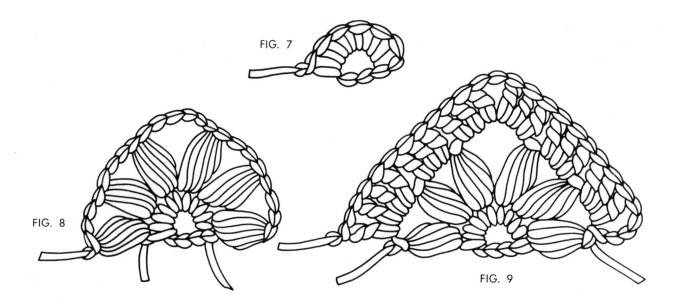

FIG. 7

FIG. 8

FIG. 9

Granny Square Five

Row 1: In Color A, ch 12, dc in sixth ch from hook, *ch 1, skip 1 ch, dc in next ch; repeat from * 2 times. Ch 4 (Figure 1). Turn.

Row 2: Dc in second dc, *ch 1, dc in next dc; repeat from *once, ch 1, dc in second ch on ch-6 loop (Figure 2). Ch 4, turn.

Row 3: *Dc in next dc, ch 1; repeat from *2 times, work last dc in second ch of ch-4. Ch 4, turn.

Row 4: Repeat Row 3. Fasten off. (Figure 3)

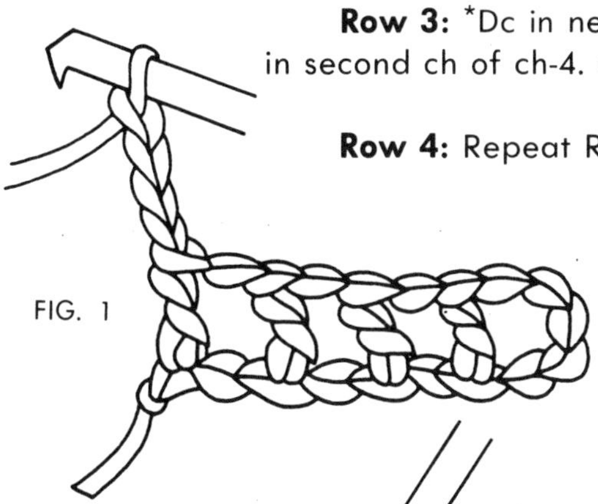

FIG. 1

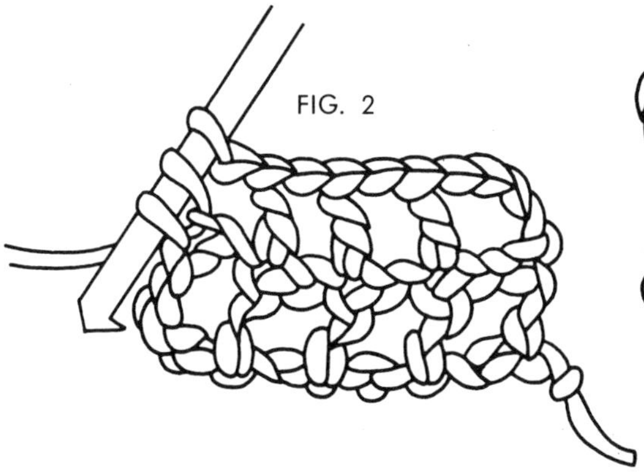

FIG. 2

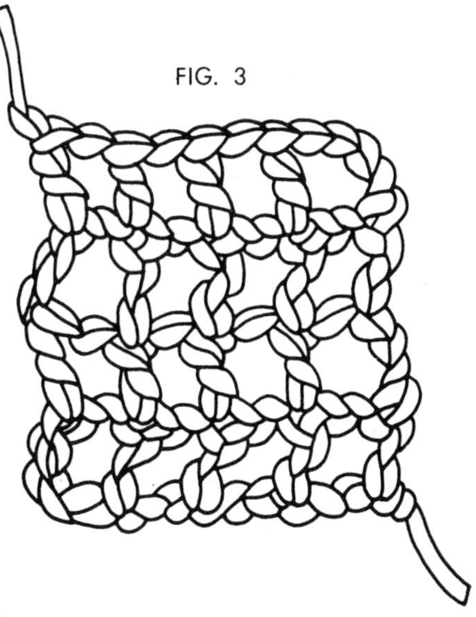

FIG. 3

Round 1: Attach Color B in any corner sp, (ch 3, 2 dc, ch 3, 3 dc) in same sp, *3 dc in each of next 2 sps, (3 dc, ch 3, 3 dc) in next corner sp (Figure 4); repeat from * 2 times, 3 dc in each of last 2 sps. Sl st to third ch of ch-3. Fasten off.

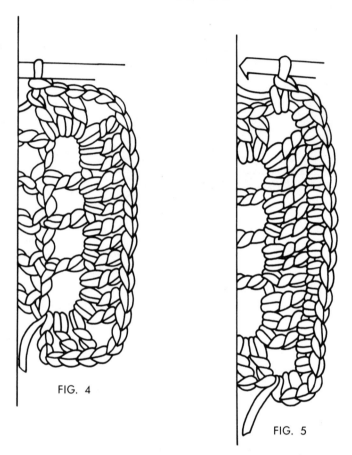

FIG. 4

FIG. 5

Round 2: Attach Color C in any ch-3 corner sp, (sc, ch 2, sc) in same sp, *sc in every dc to next corner, (sc, ch 2, sc) in next corner ch-3 sp (Figure 5); repeat from * around. Sl st to first sc made. Fasten off.

Granny Square Six

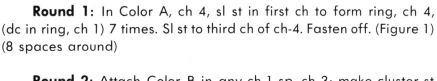

Round 1: In Color A, ch 4, sl st in first ch to form ring, ch 4, (dc in ring, ch 1) 7 times. Sl st to third ch of ch-4. Fasten off. (Figure 1) (8 spaces around)

Round 2: Attach Color B in any ch-1 sp, ch 3; make cluster st in same sp-(yo, pull up loop in sp, yo and through 2 loops on hook) 3 times (Figure 2), yo and through all 4 loops on hook, ch 1 tightly, ch 2 (Figure 3), *make cluster st in next ch-1 sp-(yo, pull up loop in sp, yo and through 2 loops on hook) 4 times, yo and through all 5 loops on hook, ch 1 tightly, ch 2; repeat from * 6 more times. Sl st to top of first cluster st. Fasten off. (Figure 4)

FIG. 1

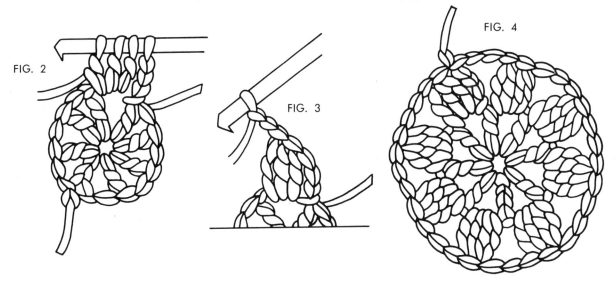

FIG. 2

FIG. 3

FIG. 4

Round 3: Attach Color C in any ch-2 sp, (ch 3, 2 dc, ch 2, 3 dc) in same sp, *3 dc in next sp, (3 dc, ch 2, 3 dc) in next sp (Figure 5); repeat from * 2 more times, 3 dc in last sp. Sl st to third ch of ch-3. Fasten off.

Round 4: Attach Color D in any dc on any side of square, sc in same st and in every st till ch-2 corner sp, *(sc, ch 2, sc) in corner, sc in every st till next corner ch-2 sp (Figure 6); repeat from * around. Sl st to first sc made. Fasten off.

FIG. 5

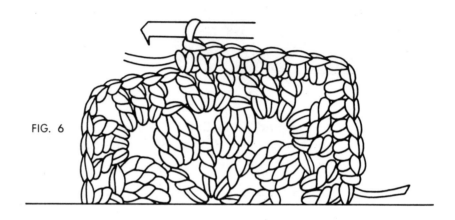

FIG. 6

Granny Square Seven

Round 1: In Color A, ch 5, sl st in first ch to form ring, ch 5, (trc in ring, ch 1) 11 times. Sl st to fourth ch of ch-5 (Figure 1). Fasten off.

Round 2: Attach Color B in any ch-1 sp, pull up loop on hook to ½″, make puff st in same sp-(yo, pull up loop in sp to ½″) 3 times (Figure 2), yo and through all 7 loops on hook, ch 1, make another

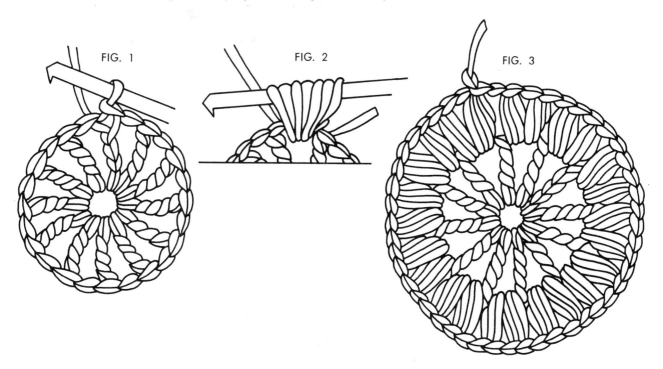

FIG. 1   FIG. 2   FIG. 3

puff st in same sp, *(puff st, ch 1, puff st, ch 1) in next sp; repeat from *10 times, sl st to top of first puff st. Fasten off. (Figure 3) (24 puff sts around)

Round 3: Attach Color C in any ch-1 sp, ch 6, trc in same sp, *ch 1, dc in next sp, (ch 1, hdc in next sp) 3 times, ch 1, dc in next sp, ch 1, (trc, ch 2, trc) in next sp (Figure 4); repeat from * around, working 2 more corners. After last dc, ch 1, sl st to fourth ch of ch-6.

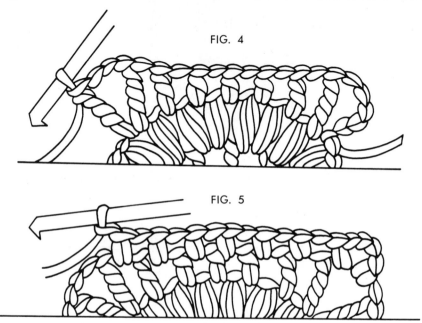

FIG. 4

FIG. 5

Round 4: Sl st into corner ch-2 sp, ch 1, (sc, ch 3, sc) in corner sp, (ch 1, sc in sp after next st) 6 times, ch 1 (Figure 5); repeat from * 3 more times. Sl st to first sc made. Fasten off.

Granny Square Eight

Round 1: In Color A, ch 6, sl st in first ch to form ring, ch 3, 3 dc in ring, drop loop from hook, insert hook in third ch of ch-3 (Figure 1), pick up dropped loop and pull through (Figure 2), ch 1 tightly (Figure 3) (popcorn st made), *ch 3, 4 dc in ring, drop loop from hook, insert hook in first of the 4 dc sts, pick up dropped loop and pull through, ch 1 tightly; repeat from * twice more, having 4 popcorn sts; ch 3. Sl st in top of first popcorn st. (Figure 4)

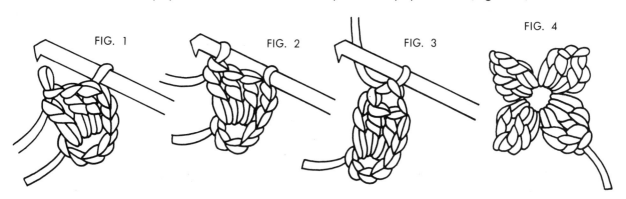

FIG. 1   FIG. 2   FIG. 3   FIG. 4

Round 2: Sl st into ch-3 sp, ch 3, 3 dc in same sp, drop loop from hook, insert hook in third ch of ch-3, pick up dropped loop and pull through, ch 1 tightly, ch 3, make another popcorn st in same sp, ch 3, *(popcorn st, ch 3, popcorn st, ch 3) in next ch-3 sp; repeat from * 2 more times. Sl st to top of first popcorn st. Fasten off. (Figure 5)

FIG. 5

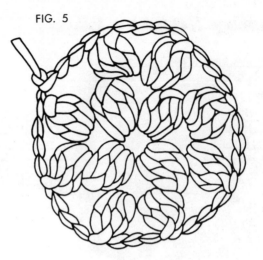

Round 3: Attach Color B in any ch-3 sp, (ch 3, 2 dc, ch 2, 3 dc) in same sp, *ch 1, 3 dc in next ch-3 sp, ch 1, (3 dc, ch 2, 3 dc) in next ch-3 sp (Figure 6); repeat from * 2 times, ch 1, 3 dc in next ch-3 sp, ch 1, sl st to third ch of ch-3. Fasten off.

FIG. 6

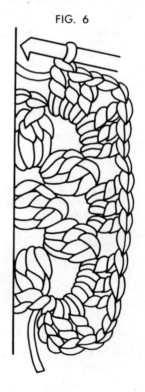

Granny Square Nine (See Bedspread, Color Plate 4)

Round 1: In Color A, ch 8, sl st in first ch to form ring, ch 3, 15 dc into ring, sl st to third ch of ch-3. (Figure 1)

Round 2: Ch 5, *dc in next dc, ch 2; repeat from * 14 times. Sl st to third ch of ch-5 (Figure 2). Fasten off. (16 spaces around)

Round 3: Attach Color B in any ch-2 sp, ch 3, 2 dc in same sp, *ch 1, 3 dc in next ch-2 sp; repeat from * 14 times, ch 1, sl st to third ch of ch-3. (Figure 3)

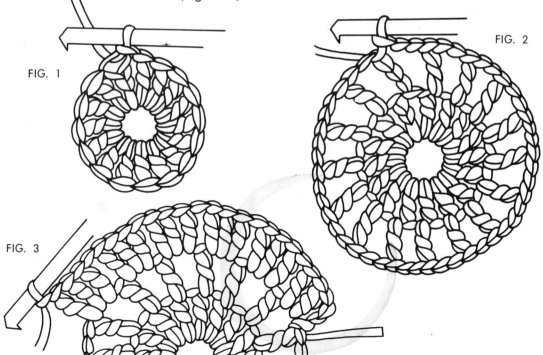

FIG. 1

FIG. 2

FIG. 3

Round 4: Sl st into next 2 dc, sc in next ch-1 sp, *ch 6, sc in next sp, (ch 3, sc in next sp) 3 times (Figure 4); repeat from * 2 times, ch 6, sc in next sp, (ch 3, sc in next sp) 2 times, ch 3. Sl st to first sc made. Fasten off.

Round 5: Attach Color C at beginning of any ch-6 sp, ch 3, (4 dc, ch 2, 5 dc) in same sp, * (3 dc in next ch-3 sp) 3 times, (5 dc, ch 2, 5 dc) in next ch-6 sp (Figure 5); repeat from * 2 times, 3 dc in each of last three ch-3 sps. Sl st to third ch of ch-3. Fasten off.

FIG. 4   FIG. 5

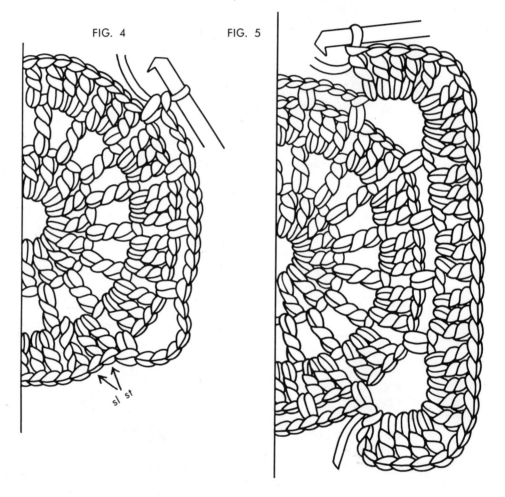

sl st

Round 6: Attach Color D in any dc on any side, ch 3, dc in next dc and in every dc till ch-2 corner sp, *(2 dc, ch 1, 2 dc) in corner sp, dc in every dc till next ch-2 corner sp; repeat from * around. Sl st to third ch of ch-3. Fasten off.

Granny Square Ten *(See Pillow, Color Plate 5)*

Round 1: In Color A, ch 12, sl st in first ch to form ring, ch 3, work 23 dc into ring, sl st to third ch of ch-3. Fasten off. (Figure 1)

Round 2: Attach Color B between any 2 dc sts, ch 1, sc in same sp, *ch 3, skip 3 dc, sc in sp after third dc (Figure 2); repeat from * 6 times, ch 3. Sl st to first sc made.

Round 3: Ch 1, sc in joining st, *work (hdc, dc, trc, dtrc, trc, dc, hdc) into ch-3 loop, sc in next sc (Figure 3); repeat from * 7 times, making 8 petals. Sl st to first sc. Fasten off.

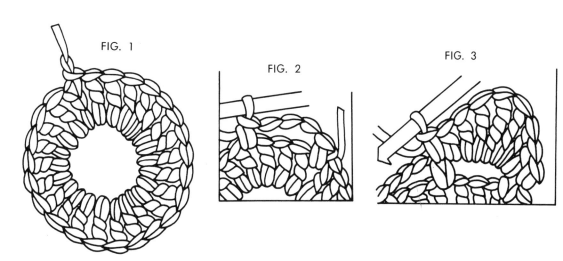

FIG. 1

FIG. 2

FIG. 3

Round 4: Attach Color C in dtrc of any petal, *ch 5, (dc, ch 3, dc) in dtrc of next petal, ch 5, sl st in dtrc of next petal (Figure 4); repeat from * 2 times, ch 5, (dc, ch 3, dc) in dtrc of next petal, ch 5. Sl st in st where yarn was attached.

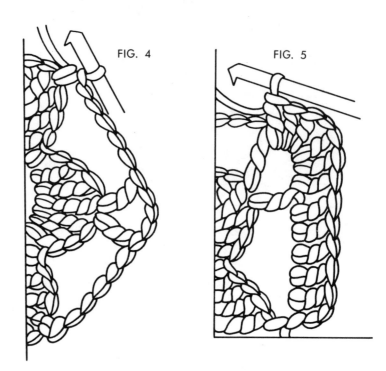

FIG. 4   FIG. 5

Round 5: Sl st into ch-5 sp, ch 3, work 5 dc in same sp, *(3 dc, ch 1, 3 dc) in corner ch-3 sp (Figure 5), 6 dc in each of next two ch-5 loops; repeat from * 2 times, (3 dc, ch 1, 3 dc) in last corner sp, 6 dc in last ch-5 loop. Sl st to third ch of ch-3. Fasten off.

Granny Square Eleven *(See Shawl, Color Plate 5)*

Round 1: In Color A, ch 4, sl st in first ch to form ring, ch 1, 8 sc into ring, sl st in first sc made. (Figure 1)

Round 2: *ch 6, sc in third ch from hook, sc in next ch, hdc in each of next 2 ch (Figure 2), sl st in next sc on ring; repeat from * 7 more times. Fasten off. (Figure 3)

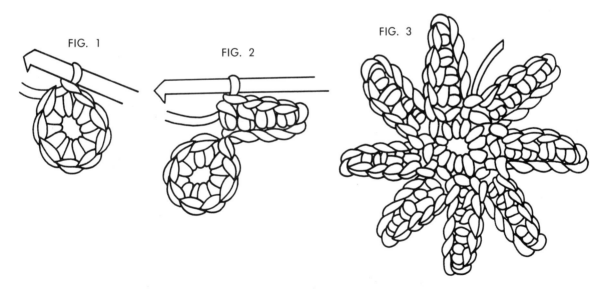

Round 3: Attach Color B in top of any petal, ch 5, dc in same sp, *ch 4, sl st in top of next petal, ch 4, (dc, ch 2, dc) in top of next

petal (Figure 4); repeat from * 2 times, ch 4, sl st in top of last petal, ch 4, sl st in third ch of ch-5. Fasten off.

Round 4: *(3 sc, ch 2, 3 sc) in corner ch-2 sp, 4 sc in ch-4 sp, skip sl st, 4 sc in next ch-4 sp (Figure 5); repeat from * 3 times. Sl st in first sc made.

Round 5: Ch 1, sc in joining st and in next 2 sc, *3 sc in corner ch-2 sp, sc in each sc to next corner (Figure 6); repeat from * around. Sl st to first sc made. Fasten off.

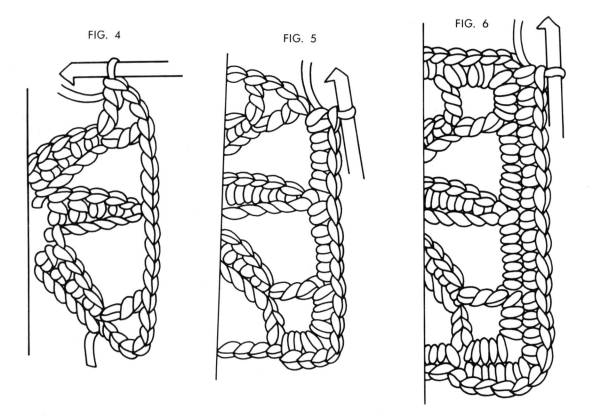

FIG. 4   FIG. 5   FIG. 6

HALF-SQUARE
To be used for shaping garments.

Round 1: Repeat Round 1 of square.

Round 2: Repeat Round 2 of square, making only 5 petals. Fasten off. (Figure 7)

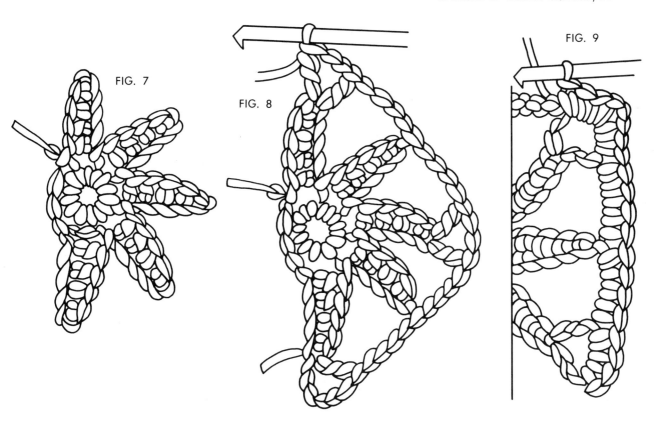

FIG. 7

FIG. 8

FIG. 9

Round 3: On same side of work, attach Color B in top of first petal, ch 5, dc in same sp, *ch 4, sl st in top of next petal, ch 4, (dc, ch 2, dc) in top of next petal; repeat from * once more (Figure 8). Ch 1, turn piece to wrong side.

Round 4: 3 sc in ch-2 sp, 4 sc in ch-4 sp, skip sl st, 4 sc in next ch-4 sp, (3 sc, ch 2, 3 sc) in ch-2 sp (Figure 9), 4 sc in ch-4 sp, skip sl st, 4 sc in ch-4 sp, 3 sc in last sp after dc. Ch 1, turn piece to right side.

Round 5: 3 sc in first sc, sc in every sc till ch-2 corner sp, 3 sc in corner sp, sc in each sc till last sc, 3 sc in last sc. Working along long side of triangle, work 3 sc in hole to right of petal, 5 sc into top of petal, 3 sc into ring, 5 sc into top of petal on other side of ring, 3 sc into hole after petal. Sl st to first sc made. Fasten off. (Figure 10)

FIG. 10

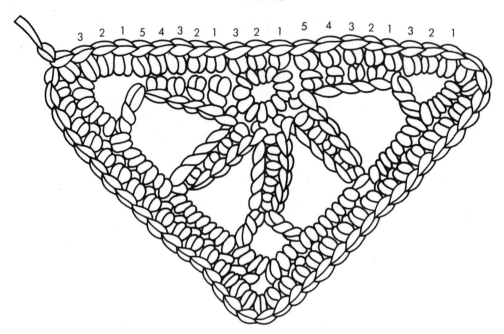

Hexagon Granny One *(See Dust Jacket.)*

Round 1: Ch 6, sl st in first ch to form ring, ch 6, (trc in ring, ch 2) 11 times. Sl st in fourth ch of ch-6. (Figure 1) (12 spaces)

Round 2: Sl st into next ch-2 sp, (ch 3, dc, ch 2, 2 dc) in same sp, 3 dc in next sp, *(2 dc, ch 2, 2 dc) in next sp, 3 dc in next sp (Figure 2); repeat from * 4 more times. Sl st in third ch of ch-3. Fasten off.

Sew motifs together into hexagon pattern as on page 156. Or, if desired, arrange colors as in afghan on dust jacket.

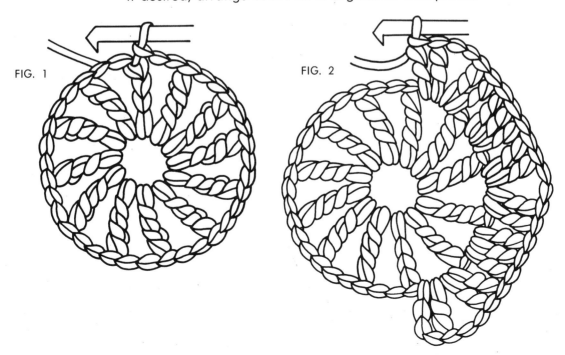

FIG. 1

FIG. 2

Hexagon Granny Two *(See Pillow, Color Plate 6)*

Round 1: In Color A, ch 5, sl st into first ch to form ring, ch 6, (dc in ring, ch 3) 5 times, ch 3, sl st in third ch of ch-6 (Figure 1). Fasten off.

FIG. 1

FIG. 2

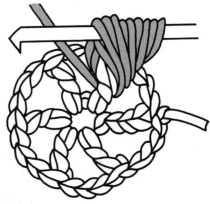

Round 2: Attach Color B in any dc, pull up loop on hook to ³⁄₄″, *(yo, insert hook under the dc st and pull through a ³⁄₄″ loop) 4 times (Figure 2), yo and through all loops on hook, ch 1 tightly, (puff st made), ch 5; repeat from * 5 times, working under every dc st around, including the ch-3. Sl st to top of first puff st (Figure 3). Fasten off.

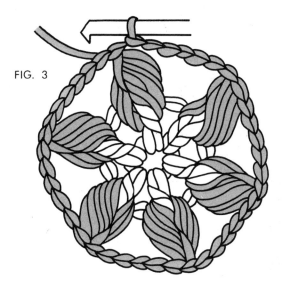

FIG. 3

Round 3: Attach Color C in any ch-5 sp, ch 3, (2 dc, ch 2, 3 dc) in same sp, *(3 dc, ch 2, 3 dc) in next sp (Figure 4); repeat from * 4 times. Sl st to third ch of ch-3. Fasten off.

Round 4: Attach Color D in any ch-2 sp, (sc, ch 2, sc) in same sp, *sc in every dc till next corner ch-2 sp, (sc, ch 2, sc) in ch-2 sp; repeat from * 4 times, sc in every remaining st. Sl st to first sc made. Fasten off.

FIG. 4

Hexagon Granny Three (See Afghan, Color Plate 2)

Round 1: In Color A, ch 9, sl st in first ch to form ring, ch 1, 18 sc into ring. Sl st to first sc made. Fasten off. (Figure 1)

Round 2: Attach Color B in any sc, ch 3, dc in each of next 2 sc, ch 6, *dc in each of next 3 sc, ch 6; repeat from * 4 more times. Sl st to third ch of ch-3. Fasten off. (Figure 2)

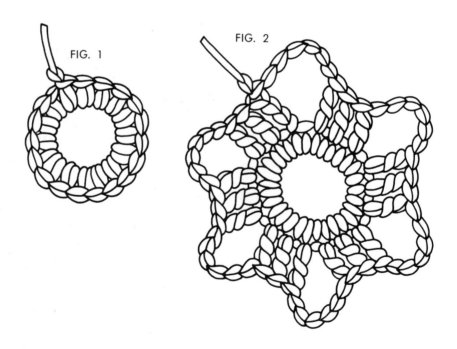

FIG. 1

FIG. 2

Round 3: Attach Color C in any first dc of any 3-dc group, ch 3, 2 dc in next dc, dc in third dc, ch 4, *in next 3-dc group work dc in first dc, 2 dc in second dc, dc in third dc, ch 4 (Figure 3); repeat from * 4 more times. Sl st to third ch of ch-3. Fasten off.

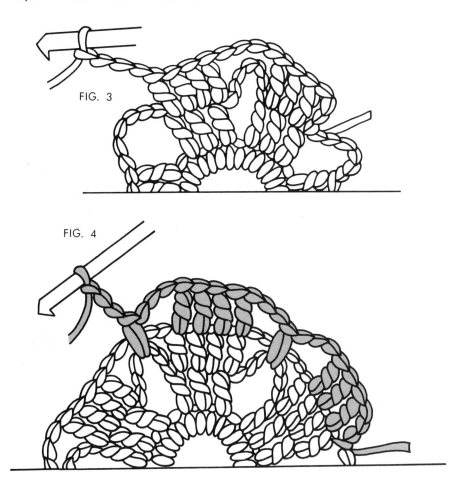

FIG. 3

FIG. 4

Round 4: Attach Color D in first dc of any 4-dc group, ch 3, dc in each of next 3 dc, ch 3, sc *loosely* over the 2 chain loops below, ch 3, *dc in each of next 4 dc, ch 3, sc *loosely* over the 2 chain loops below, ch 3 (Figure 4); repeat from * 4 more times. Sl st in third ch of ch-3. Fasten off.

Attach hexagon motifs together as in photograph, sewing together the 4-dc groups *only* for an openwork effect.

Hexagon Granny Four

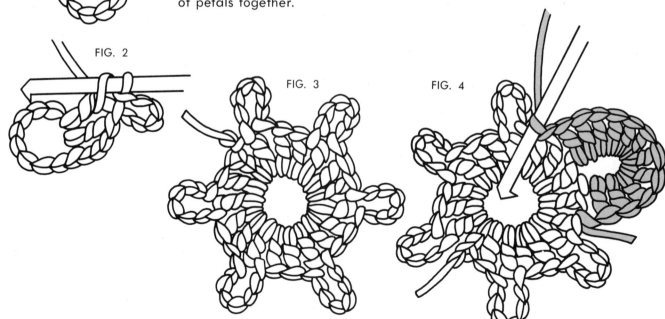

FIG. 1

FIG. 2

FIG. 3

FIG. 4

Round 1: In Color A, ch 9, sl st in first ch to form ring, ch 3, 2 dc in ring, *ch 6 (Figure 1), sl st sideways in last dc made (Figure 2), 3 dc in ring; repeat from * 4 times, ch 6, sl st in last dc, sl st in third ch of ch-3. Fasten off.

Round 2: Attach Color B in any center dc of any 3-dc group, *work 11 dc sts into ch-6 loop, sl st in center dc of next 3-dc group (Figure 4); repeat from * 5 times. Sl st in st where yarn was attached. Fasten off.

Sew motifs together as in photograph, sewing top edge stitches of petals together.

Circular Granny One

Round 1: Ch 6, sl st in first ch to form ring, ch 5, (dc in ring, ch 2) 7 times, sl st in third ch of ch-6. (Figure 1)

Round 2: Ch 1, sc in joining st, *2 sc in ch-2 sp, sc in dc; repeat from * 6 times, 2 sc in last sp. Sl st in first sc made (Figure 2) (24 sc sts around). Fasten off here or continue to enlarge circle.

Round 3: Ch 4, *dc in next sc, ch 1; repeat from * 22 times, ch 1, sl st to third ch of ch-4. (Figure 3) (24 spaces)

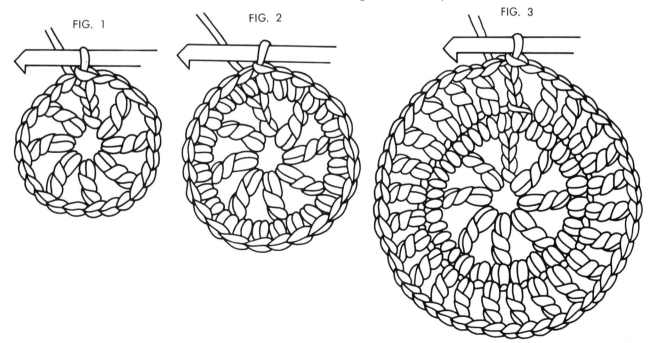

FIG. 1   FIG. 2   FIG. 3

Round 4: Ch 1, sc in joining st, *sc in ch-1 sp, sc in dc; repeat from * 22 times, sc in last sp. Sl st to first sc made (Figure 4). (48 sc around) Fasten off here or continue to enlarge.

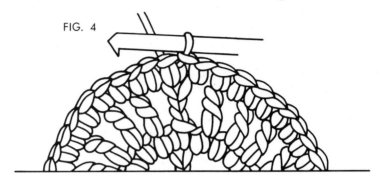

FIG. 4

Round 5: Ch 5, *skip 1 sc, dc in next sc, ch 2; repeat from * 22 times. Sl st to third ch of ch-5. (Figure 5) (24 spaces around)

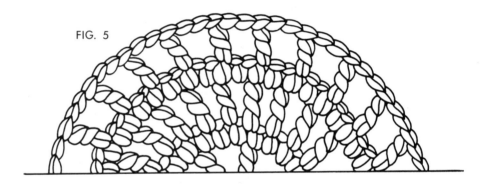

FIG. 5

Round 6: Ch 1, sc in joining st, *2 sc in ch-2 sp, sc in dc; repeat from * 22 times, 2 sc in last ch-2 sp. Sl st in first sc made (Figure 6). Fasten off.

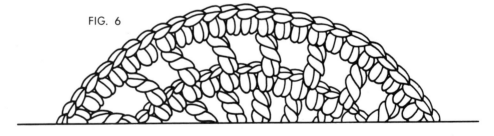

FIG. 6

Make motifs in all three sizes. Arrange and sew together as in photograph.

Circular Granny Two *(See Afghan, Color Plate 7)*

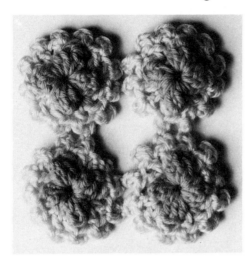

Round 1: In Color A, ch 5, sl st in first ch to form ring, ch 3, 3 dc in ring, take hook out of loop, insert it in third ch of ch-3 (Figure 1), pull dropped loop through space (Figure 2), ch 1 tightly (Figure 3), ch 2, * 4 dc in ring, take hook out of loop, insert it in first dc, pull dropped loop through it, ch 1 tightly (popcorn st made), ch 2; repeat from * 2 more times. Sl st to top of first popcorn st. Fasten off. (Figure 4)

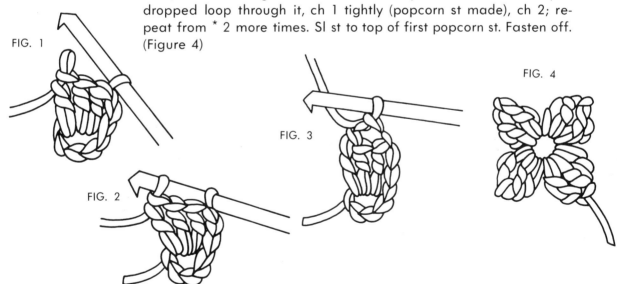

FIG. 1

FIG. 2

FIG. 3

FIG. 4

Round 2: Attach Color B in any ch-2 sp, (ch 4, dc, ch 1, dc) in same sp, *(ch 1, dc) 3 times in next sp; repeat from * 2 times, ch 1, sl st to third ch of ch-4 (Figure 5).

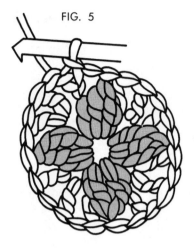

FIG. 5

Round 3: Ch 5, *trc in next dc, ch 1; repeat from * 10 times (Figure 6), ch 1, sl st in fourth ch of ch-5.

FIG. 6

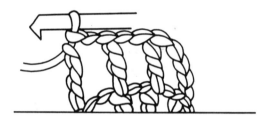

Round 4: Ch 3, work dc in each trc around (Figure 7). Sl st to third ch of ch-3. Fasten off.

FIG. 7

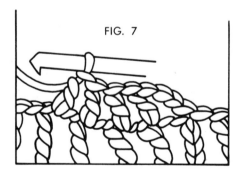

A three-dimensional effect will be formed, with the popcorn stitches protruding. Attach motifs together as in photograph.

Triangular Granny One

Round 1: In Color A, ch 6, sl st in first ch to form ring, ch 4, (dc in ring, ch 1) 11 times. Sl st to third ch of ch-4. Fasten off. (Figure 1)

Round 2: Attach Color B in any ch-1 sp, ch 4, *(trc, ch 7, trc) in next sp, (ch 1, dc in next sp) 3 times, ch 1 (Figure 2); repeat from * once more, (trc, ch 7, trc) in next sp, (ch 1, dc in next sp) 2 times, ch 1, sl st to third ch of ch-4. Fasten off.

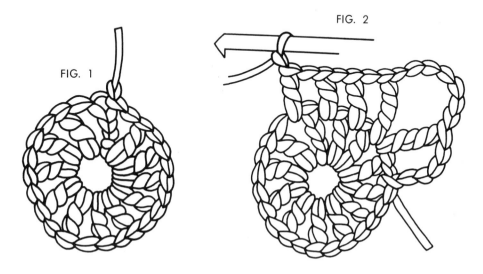

FIG. 2

FIG. 1

Round 3: Attach Color C in the ch-1 sp before any corner trc, sc in same sp, *ch 1, (sc, ch 1, sc, ch 5, sc, ch 1, sc) in corner ch-7 sp, (ch 1, sc in next ch-1 sp) 4 times (Figure 3); repeat from * once more, ch 1, (sc, ch 1, sc, ch 5, sc, ch 1, sc) in next sp, (ch 1, sc in next ch-1 sp) 3 times, ch 1, sl st to first sc made. Fasten off.

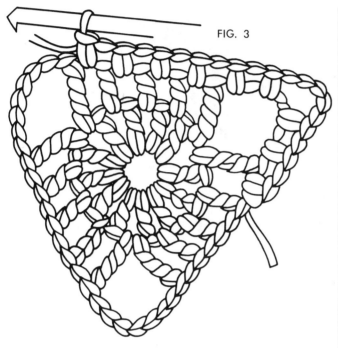

FIG. 3

Shawl based on Triangular Granny One.
Made of Fruit-of-the-Loom yarn.

Attach motifs together as in photograph.

3

Nostalgic Grannies

Throughout Victorian times and halfway into the Twentieth Century, crocheting was used to make decorative interior fabrics for table coverings and furniture embellishments. Materials used for crochet at that time were generally fine cotton and silk threads, rather than heavier wool and synthetic blend yarns that we use today. Every home had its share of delicate doilies placed on tables and antimacassars on furniture to protect it from soiling. Delicate trimmings, such as collars, cuffs, and hems, were also crocheted in fine cotton yarns and then applied as embellishments to garments. Today, there is a resurgence of interest in the delicacy and nostalgic charm of this fine crochet work, even though this kind of handwork requires large amounts of time and care.

The instructions for some of the intricate, lacy patterns of yesteryear are very lengthy and would often fill many pages in women's magazines and pattern books of the day. The eight patchwork crochet patterns in this chapter are much simpler versions of these historic patterns, but they capture the same exquisite, gauzy texture.

81

Most of the motifs are technically granny squares, since most are worked from the center out, but with much more complexity and variety of texture. These motifs are very cleverly designed — as single units, they have a distinct, attractive pattern; but when attached to a group of identical motifs, they create an enchanting, multipatterned texture.

As you glance through the chapter, notice the similarity of these designs to those you may have come across in museums, historic restorations, and antique shops. Included here is a filet crochet pattern, which was very popular for use as a trim insertion on sheets and pillowcases and two hexagonal patterns which were often made into bedspreads.

As in the past, what determines the delicacy of this type of work is the material used to make it. The preferred yarns are crochet cotton, sport-weight yarn, baby yarn, or any other fine yarn. Such novelty yarns as straw and metallic yarns can be used to give these traditional motifs a contemporary look. The colors that show off the pattern to the best advantage are white, black, ecru, or other neutral shades. The fine, gauzy texture created with these motifs is suitable for making tablecloths, placemats, bedspreads, lampshades, curtains, room dividers, shawls, eveningwear, or any other home or fashion item that should have a dainty, quaint feeling.

Nostalgic Granny One

Right:
Nostalgic Granny One
Left:
Nostalgic Granny Two

Round 1: Ch 5, sl st in first ch to form ring, ch 1, 8 sc in ring, sl st in first sc made. (Figure 1)

Round 2: Ch 4; keeping last loop of each of the following stitches on hook, work 3 trc in joining st of last round (Figure 2), yo and through all 4 loops on hook (Figure 3), ch 4 (Figure 4), *keeping last loop of each of the following stitches on hook, work 4 trc in next sc, yo and through all 5 loops on hook, ch 4 (cluster st

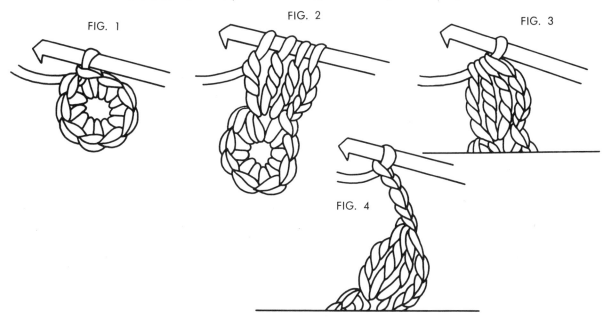

FIG. 1

FIG. 2

FIG. 3

FIG. 4

made); repeat from * 4 more times working 8 cluster stitches around. Sl st to top of first cluster. (Figure 5)

FIG. 5

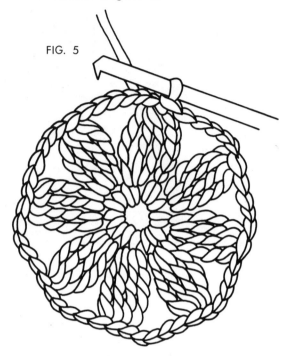

Round 3: Ch 1, sc in top of first cluster, *4 sc in ch-4 sp, sc in top of next cluster (Figure 6); repeat from * around. Sl st to first sc. Fasten off.

FIG. 6

To join, sew flat sides of motifs together, as pictured in table mat.

Nostalgic Granny Two

Work Rounds 1, 2, and 3 as for Nostalgic Granny One. Do not fasten off yarn at end of Round 3.

Round 4: *ch 4, skip 1 sc, sc in next sc; repeat from * around (Figure 1). Sl st at bottom of first ch-4 loop. (20 meshes)

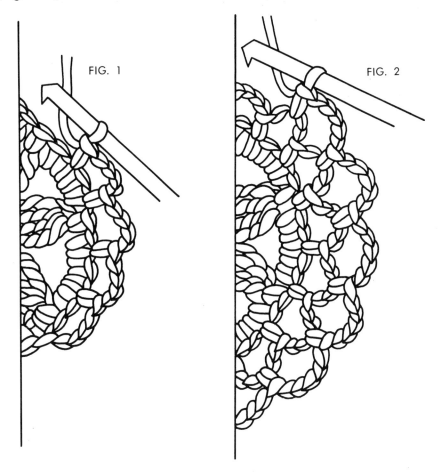

FIG. 1

FIG. 2

Round 5: Ch 1, sc into first mesh, *ch 5, sc in next mesh (Figure 2); repeat from * around. Sl st in first sc made into first mesh. Fasten off.

To join, sew 2 matching meshes of 2 motifs together. Skip 3 meshes on one motif. Sew another motif to it, attaching next 2 meshes. Sew a few strips of desired number of motifs. Attach strips together, sewing each matching 2 meshes on sides together, as pictured in table mat, page 83.

Nostalgic Granny Three

Left: *Nostalgic Granny Three*
Right: *Nostalgic Granny Three (enlarged)*

Round 1: Ch 2, 6 sc in second ch from hook. (Figure 1)

Round 2: Sc in first sc made, *ch 3, sc in next sc; repeat from * 4 times, ch 3. (Figure 2)

Round 3: 2 sc in first ch-3 loop, *ch 3, 2 sc in next ch-3 loop; repeat from * 4 times, ch 3. (Figure 3)

Round 4: *Skip next sc, sc in next sc, 2 sc in ch-3 loop, ch 3; repeat from * 5 more times. (Figure 4)

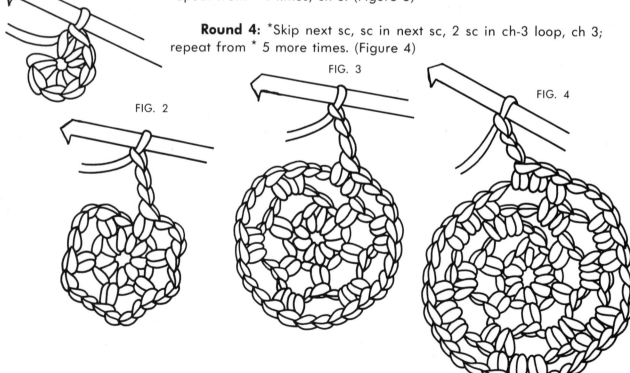

FIG. 1

FIG. 2

FIG. 3

FIG. 4

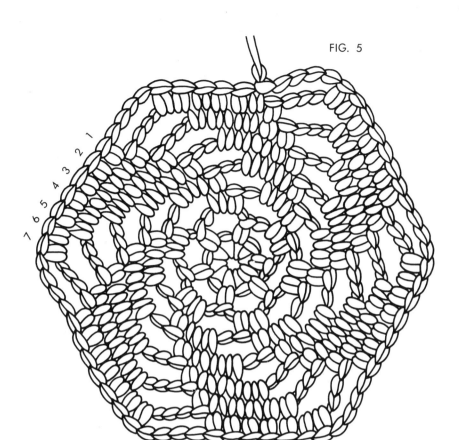

FIG. 5

Round 5: *Skip next sc, sc in each of next 2 sc, 2 sc in ch-3 loop, ch 4; repeat from * 5 more times.

Round 6: *Skip next sc, sc in each of next 3 sc, 2 sc in ch-3 loop, ch 4; repeat from * 5 more times.

Continue working as for Round 6, increasing 1 sc on each section on each round and chaining 4 between sections, till there are 7 sc stitches on each section. TO END MOTIF HERE: Ch 4, skip first sc on next section, sl st in next sc. Fasten off. (Figure 5)

To join, arrange numerous motifs together to form hexagon pattern, as on page 86, and sew only the sc stitches of adjoining sections together, not the chain loops.

To enlarge motif for using it singly, as in table mat, proceed as follows.

When there are 7 sc stitches on each section, begin chaining 5 between sections. When there are 11 sc stitches on each section, begin chaining 6 between sections. When there are 15 sc stitches on each section, begin chaining 7 between sections. When there are 17 sc stitches on each section, begin chaining 8 between sections. When there are 19 sc stitches on each section, begin chaining 9 between sections.

Nostalgic Granny Four

Round 1: Ch 6, sl st in first ch to form ring, ch 3, 11 dc in ring, sl st to third ch of ch-3. (Figure 1)

FIG. 1

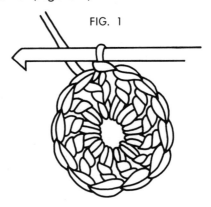

Round 2: Ch 3, dc in joining, 2 dc in next dc, *ch 1, 2 dc in each of next 2 dc; repeat from * 4 times. Ch 1, sl st to third ch of ch-3. (Figure 2)

FIG. 2

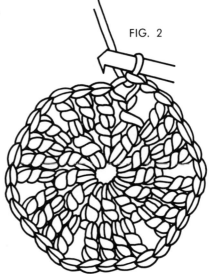

Round 3: Ch 3, dc in joining, dc in each of next 2 dc, 2 dc in third dc, *ch 2, 2 dc in next dc, dc in each of next 2 dc, 2 dc in next dc; repeat from * 4 times. Ch 2, sl st to third ch of ch-3. (Figure 3)

FIG. 3

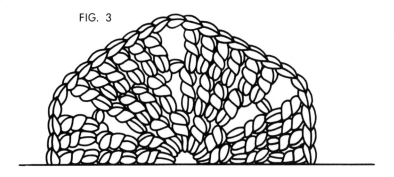

Round 4: Ch 3, dc in joining, dc in each of next 4 dc, 2 dc in last dc of section, *ch 3, 2 dc in first dc of next section, dc in each of next 4 dc, 2 dc in last dc of section; repeat from * 4 times. Ch 3, sl st to third ch of ch-3.

Round 5: Ch 3, dc in joining, dc in each of next 6 dc, 2 dc in last dc of section, *ch 4, 2 dc in first dc of next section, dc in each of next 6 dc, 2 dc in last dc of section; repeat from * 4 times. Ch 4, sl st to third ch of ch-3. Fasten off here or continue to add one or two more rounds.

Round 6: Ch 3, dc in joining, dc in each of next 8 dc, 2 dc in last dc of section, *ch 5, 2 dc in first dc of next section, dc in each of next 8 dc, 2 dc in last dc of section; repeat from * 4 times. Ch 5, sl st to third ch of ch-3.

Round 7: Ch 3, dc in joining, dc in each of next 10 dc, 2 dc in last dc of section, *ch 6, 2 dc in first dc of next section, dc in each of next 10 dc, 2 dc in last dc of section; repeat from * 4 times. Ch 6, sl st to third ch of ch-3. Fasten off.

To join, arrange motifs in hexagon pattern as on page 94 and sew dc stitches of adjoining motifs together, not the chain loops.

Nostalgic Granny Five

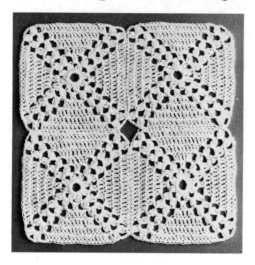

Round 1: Ch 8, sl st in first ch to form ring, ch 3; keeping on hook last loop of each st, make 2 dc in ring (Figure 1), yo and through all 3 loops on hook, ch 1 tightly, ch 2 (Figure 2), *keeping on hook last loops of each st, make 3 dc in ring (Figure 3), yo and through all 4 loops on hook, ch 1 tightly, ch 2 (Figure 4); repeat from * 6 times. Sl st to top of first cluster st. (Figure 5)

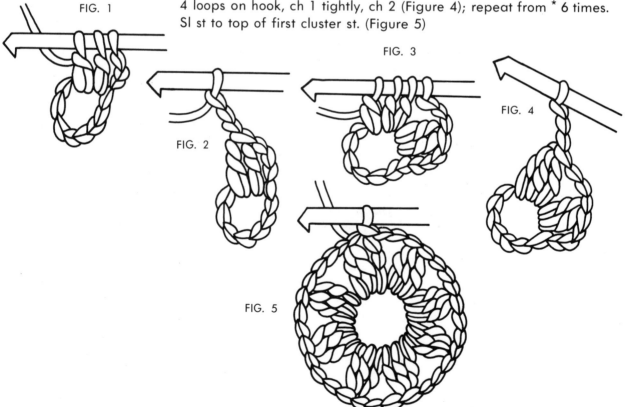

FIG. 1

FIG. 2

FIG. 3

FIG. 4

FIG. 5

NOTE: When doing the cluster st, you always ch 1 tightly after the st, then ch 2, 3, or number indicated for spacing between the sts. The "ch 1 tightly" will not be mentioned from now on.

Round 2: Sl st into next ch-2 sp, ch 3, work cluster st in same sp as at the beginning of Round 1, ch 3, make another cluster st in same sp, ch 1, *2 dc in next sp, ch 2, (cluster st, ch 3, cluster st) in next sp (Figure 6); repeat from * around. Sl st to top of first cluster st.

Round 3: Sl st into corner ch-3 sp, ch 3, work (cluster st, ch 3, cluster st) in same sp, *ch 1, 2 dc in ch-1 sp, dc in each of next 2 dc, 2 dc in ch-2 sp, ch 2, (cluster st, ch 3, cluster st) in next corner sp (Figure 7); repeat from * around. Sl st to top of first cluster st.

Round 4: Sl st into corner ch-3 sp, ch 3, (cluster st, ch 3, cluster st) in same sp, *ch 1, 2 dc in ch-1 sp, dc in each dc till ch-2 sp, 2 dc in ch-2 sp, ch 2, (cluster st, ch 3, cluster st) in next corner sp (Figure 8); repeat from * around. Sl st to top of first cluster st.

Rounds 5 and 6: Repeat Round 4. Fasten off.

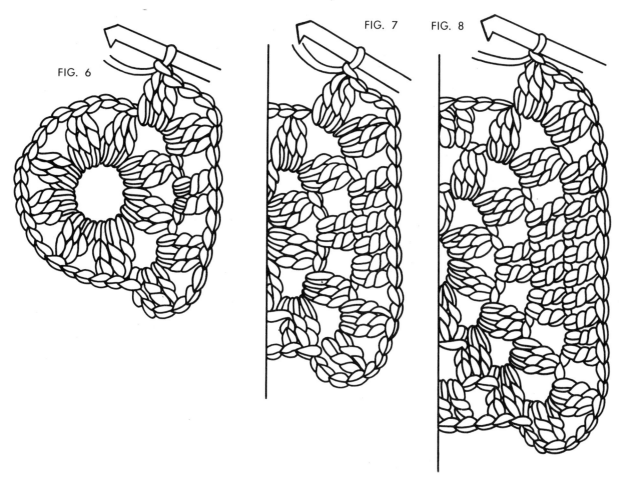

FIG. 6

FIG. 7   FIG. 8

Nostalgic Granny Six

Round 1: Ch 5, sl st in first ch to form ring, ch 1, 8 sc into ring. Sl st to first sc made. (Figure 1)

Round 2: Ch 5, *dc in next sc, ch 2; repeat from * until 7 spaces are made, ch 2, sl st to third ch of ch-5. (Figure 2) (8 spaces)

Round 3: Ch 1, sc in joining st, *3 sc in ch-2 sp, sc in dc; repeat from * around. Sl st to first sc made. (Figure 3)

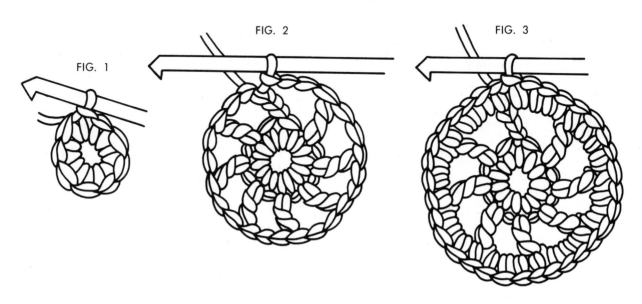

FIG. 1   FIG. 2   FIG. 3

Round 4: Ch 1, sc in same sp, *ch 7, skip 3 sc, sc in next st (Figure 4); repeat from * around. Sl st to first sc. (8 loops)

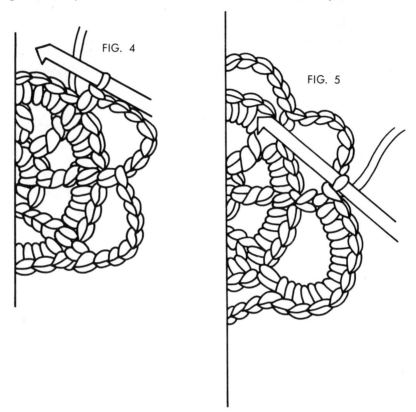

FIG. 4

FIG. 5

Round 5: *Work 9 sc in loop, sl st in sc (Figure 5); repeat from * around. Sl st in last sc. Fasten off.

Sew motifs together as pictured.

Nostalgic Granny Seven

Left:
Nostalgic Granny Four
Right:
Nostalgic Granny Seven

Round 1: Ch 10, sl st in first ch to form ring, ch 7, *5 trc into ring, ch 3; repeat from * 2 times, 4 trc into ring, sl st to fourth ch of ch-7. (Figure 1)

Round 2: Sl st into corner sp, ch 5, (trc, ch 1) 7 times into same sp, *(trc, ch 1) 8 times into next corner sp; repeat from * twice. Sl st to fourth ch of ch-5. (Figure 2)

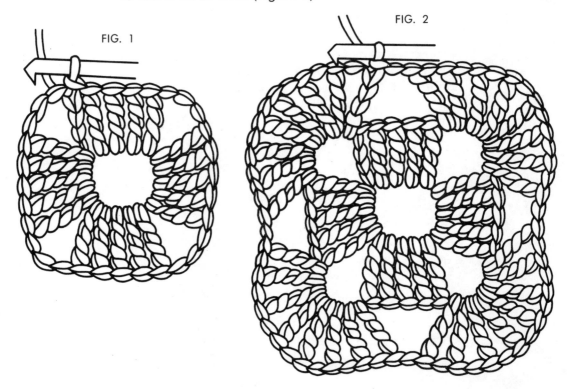

FIG. 1

FIG. 2

Round 3: Ch 1, sc in same st, sc in next ch-1 sp, *sc in next trc, (sc, ch 1, sc) in next ch-1 sp, (sc in next trc, sc in next ch-1 sp) 3 times, sc in next trc, (sc, ch 1, sc) in next ch-1 sp, (sc in next trc, sc in next ch-1 sp) 3 times (Figure 3); repeat from * around. Sl st to first sc made. Fasten off.

FIG. 3

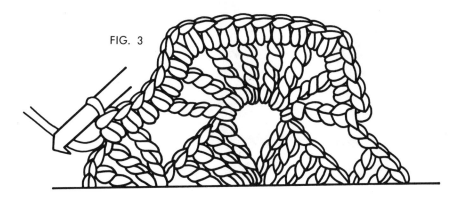

Attach motifs by sewing together matching flat sides of ad-joining motifs so that open areas between will form circular shapes.

Nostalgic Granny Eight

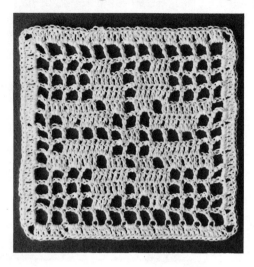

Chain 44.

Row 1: Dc in eighth ch from hook, *ch 2, sk 2 chs, dc in next ch; repeat from * across. Ch 5, turn. (Figure 1) (13 sps across)

FIG. 1

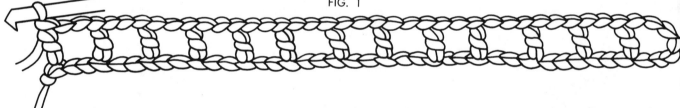

Row 2: Dc in second dc, (ch 2, dc in next dc) 3 times, 2 dc in next ch-2 sp, dc in next dc, (ch 2, dc in next dc) 3 times, 2 dc in ch-2 sp, dc in next dc, (ch 2, dc in next dc) 3 times, ch 2, dc in third ch on ch-8 (Figure 2). Ch 5, turn.

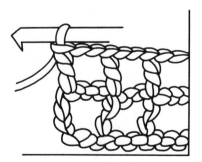

FIG. 2

Row 3: Dc in second dc, (ch 2, dc in next dc) 3 times, dc in next 3 dc, 2 dc in ch-2 sp, dc in dc, ch 2, dc in next dc, 2 dc in ch-2 sp, dc in each of next 4 dc, (ch 2, dc in next dc) 3 times, ch 2, dc in third ch of ch-5. Ch 5, turn.

Row 4: Dc in second dc, (ch 2, dc in next dc) 3 times, dc in next 6 dc, ch 2, dc in next 7 dc, (ch 2, dc in next dc) 3 times, ch 2, dc in third ch of ch-5. Ch 5, turn.

Row 5: Dc in second dc, (2 dc in ch-2 sp, dc in next dc) 3 times, ch 2, skip 2 dc, dc in each of next 4 dc, ch 2, dc in each of next 4 dc, ch 2, skip 2 dc, (dc in next dc, 2 dc in ch-2 sp) 3 times, dc in next dc, ch 2, dc in third ch of ch-5. Ch 5, turn.

Row 6: Dc in second dc, ch 2, skip 2 dc, dc in each of next 7 dc, 2 dc in ch-2 sp, dc in next dc, ch 2, skip 2 dc, dc in next dc, ch 2, dc in next dc, ch 2, skip 2 dc, dc in next dc, 2 dc in ch-2 sp, dc in each of next 7 dc, ch 2, skip 2 dc, dc in next dc, ch 2, dc in third ch of ch-5. Ch 5, turn.

Row 7: Dc in second dc, ch 2, dc in next dc, (ch 2, skip 2 dc, dc in next dc) 3 times, ch 2, dc in next dc, 2 dc in ch-2 sp, dc in dc, ch 2, dc in next dc, (ch 2, skip 2 dc, dc in next dc) 3 times, ch 2, dc in next dc, ch 2, dc in third ch of ch-5. Ch 5, turn.

FIG. 3

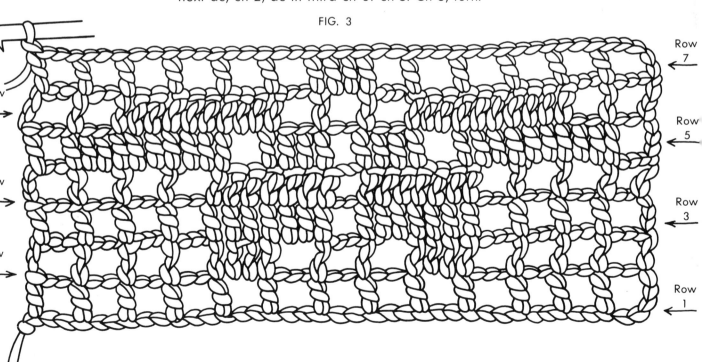

Row 7

Row 5

Row 3

Row 1

Row 8: Dc in second dc, ch 2, dc in next dc, (2 dc in ch-2 sp, dc in next dc) 3 times, ch 2, dc in next dc, ch 2, skip 2 dc, dc in next dc, ch 2, dc in next dc, (2 dc in ch-2 sp, dc in next dc) 3 times, ch 2, dc in next dc, ch 2, dc in third ch of ch-5. Ch 5, turn.

Row 9: Dc in second dc, 2 dc in next ch-2 sp, dc in each of next 7 dc, ch 2, skip 2 dc, dc in next dc, 2 dc in ch-2 sp, dc in next dc, ch 2, dc in next dc, 2 dc in ch-2 sp, dc in next dc, ch 2, skip 2 dc, dc in each of next 7 dc, 2 dc in ch-2 sp, dc in next dc, ch 2, dc in third ch of ch-5. Ch 5, turn.

Row 10: Dc in second dc, (ch 2, skip 2 dc, dc in next dc) 3 times, 2 dc in ch-2 sp, dc in each of next 4 dc, ch 2, dc in each of next 4 dc, 2 dc in ch-2 sp, dc in next dc, (ch 2, skip 2 dc, dc in next dc) 3 times, ch 2, dc in third ch of ch-5. Ch 5, turn.

Row 11: Dc in second dc, (ch 2, dc in next dc) 3 times, dc in each of next 6 dc, ch 2, dc in each of next 7 dc, (ch 2, dc in next dc) 3 times, ch 2, dc in third ch of ch-5. Ch 5, turn.

Row 12: Dc in second dc, (ch 2, dc in next dc) 3 times, dc in each of next 3 dc, ch 2, skip 2 dc, dc in next dc, ch 2, dc in next dc, ch 2, skip 2 dc, dc in next 4 dc, (ch 2, dc in next dc) 3 times, ch 2, dc in third ch of ch-5. Ch 5, turn.

Row 13: Dc in second dc, (ch 2, dc in next dc) 3 times, ch 2, skip 2 dc, dc in next dc, (ch 2, dc in next dc) 3 times, ch 2, skip 2 dc, dc in next dc, (ch 2, dc in next dc) 3 times, ch 2, dc in third ch of ch-5. Fasten off.

For edging, attach yarn in any mesh on any side. Ch 3, 2 dc in same sp, * work 3 dc in every sp till corner sp, (3 dc, ch 3, 3 dc) in corner; repeat from * around (Figure 3). Sl st to third ch of ch-3. Fasten off.

FIG. 4

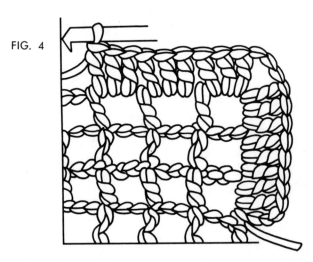

4

Graphic Grannies

In the past, yarns for crocheting, knitting, and other crafts were often dyed with vegetable dyes. The colors that resulted were the berry tints, the earth tones, and other soft, subtle shades. Today yarns appear in a tremendous variety of colors and there is an emphasis on the strong, intense "happy" colors. By crocheting these colors in the patchwork technique, you can very effectively capture the crispness and vibrancy of geometric design appearing in poster art and modernistic home decor.

A departure from the traditional, multitextured granny square and the delicate, nostalgic granny, the following eight Graphic Grannies are all made with basic flat stitches for a solid, vivid effect. Though each forms a standard geometric shape, not every one is worked from the center out, some are worked in rows. Each is designed to accommodate a few colors. Done in a solid color, a graphic granny loses its impact.

The primary and secondary colors of the spectrum, such as red, blue, yellow, orange, green, and purple, produce the most graphic look. In most projects made of graphic grannies, you would use a neutral shade as white, off-white, or black to blend and neutralize these blazing crayon colors. With a little imagination you could arrange a group of multicolored graphic grannies to create unusual, eye-catching effects, perhaps even to duplicate a striking contemporary slipcover or wallpaper pattern in your home.

The Graphic Grannies may be executed effectively in any sort of yarn from rug and worsted-weight yarn to cotton and straw yarn. They can be made into a variety of articles. Children's and infants' afghans are a natural, since youngsters are often dazzled by bright, crisp colors and shapes. Crocheted in somewhat more placid color combinations, the Graphic Grannies can be made into rugs, bedspreads, garments, and accessories.

Graphic Granny One

Graphic Granny One   Graphic Granny Two   Graphic Granny Three

Round 1: In Color A, ch 4, sl st in first ch to form ring, ch 3, 11 dc in ring (12 dc). Sl st to third ch of ch-3. Fasten off. (Figure 1)

Round 2: Attach Color B in any dc, ch 3, dc in same st, work 2 dc in each dc around (24 dc). Sl st to third ch of ch-3. Fasten off. (Figure 2)

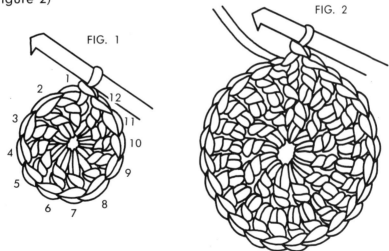

Round 3: Attach Color C in any dc, ch 3, dc in same st, *dc in next dc, 2 dc in next dc; repeat from * around (36 dc). Sl st to third ch of ch-3. Fasten off.

Graphic Granny Two (See Pillow, Color Plate 7)

Round 1: Work same as for Round 1 of Graphic Granny One.

Round 2: Attach Color B in any dc, ch 3, 4 dc in same st, *dc in next 2 dc, in third dc work 5 dc; repeat from * two times, dc in last 2 dc, sl st to third ch of ch-3. Fasten off. (Figure 1)

FIG. 1

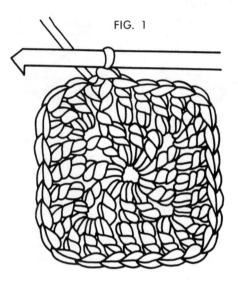

Round 3: Attach Color C in any side dc st, ch 3, *dc in next dc and every dc till corner dc (third dc of the 5-dc group of the previous round), 5 dc in corner dc; repeat from * around. Sl st to third ch of ch-3. Fasten off.

Graphic Granny Three (See Pillow, Color Plate 7)

Work Rounds 1, 2, and 3 as for Graphic Granny One.

Round 4: Attach Color D in any dc st, ch 4, 4 trc in same st, *in next 8 sts work dc, 6 hdc, dc, 5 trc in next st (Figure 1); repeat from * around. Sl st to fourth ch of ch-4.

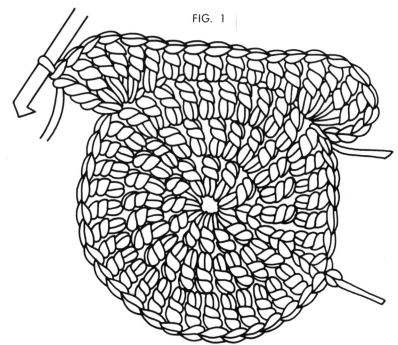

FIG. 1

Round 5: Ch 3, dc in next dc and every dc till corner trc st (center trc of 5-trc group), *5 dc into corner trc st, dc in every st till next corner trc (Figure 2); repeat from * around. Sl st to third ch of ch-3. Fasten off.

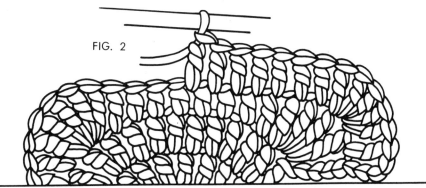

FIG. 2

Graphic Granny Four _(See Afghan, Color Plate 2)_

Round 1: Ch 4, sl st in first ch to form ring, ch 1, *sc in ring, ch 2; repeat from * 3 more times. Sl st to first sc. (Figure 1)

Round 2: Sl st into corner ch-2 sp, ch 1, (sc, ch 2, sc) in same sp, ch 1 (Figure 2), *(sc, ch 2, sc) in next corner sp, ch 1; repeat from * twice more. Sl st to first sc.

FIG. 1

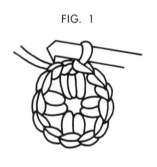

FIG. 2

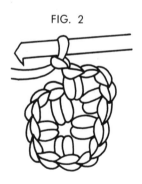

FIG. 3

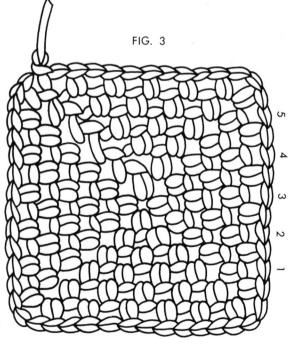

Round 3: Sl st into corner ch-2 sp, ch 1, *(sc, ch 2, sc) in corner sp, ch 1, sc in ch-1 sp, ch 1; repeat from * around. Sl st to first sc.

Round 4: Sl st into corner ch-2 sp, ch 1, *(sc, ch 2, sc) in corner sp, (ch 1, sc) in every ch-1 sp till next corner, ch 1; repeat from * around. Sl st to first sc.

Repeat Round 4 as many times as desired, changing colors wherever desired. (Figure 3)

To change colors after making sl st to end round, fasten off yarn and attach new color in any one of the 4 corners. Work round regularly.

To form diamond-in-a-square effect, end diamond on a round where there are an odd number of ch-1 sps on each side (not counting corner ch-2 sps). Each triangular side is crocheted as follows.

Row 1: Attach contrasting color yarn in ch-2 corner sp, sc in same sp, *ch 1, sc in next sp; repeat from * across side of diamond, working last sc in next corner (Figure 4). Ch 1, turn.

Row 2: (Sc, ch 1) in every ch-1 sp across, sc in last sp. Ch 1, turn.

Repeat Row 2 till there are no more spaces left, working last sc in last sp at point. Fasten off. (Figure 5)

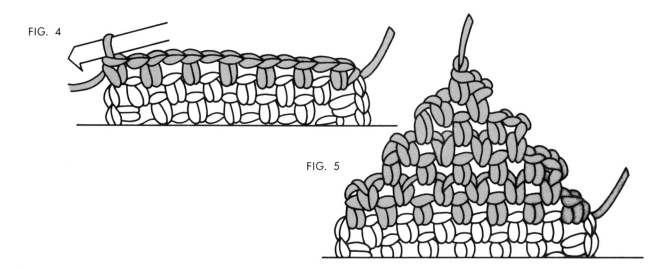

FIG. 4

FIG. 5

Graphic Granny Five (See Two Pillows, Color Plate 5)

Round 1: In Color A, ch 4, sl st in first ch to form ring, ch 3, 11 dc in ring, sl st to third ch of ch-3. Fasten off. (Figure 1)

Round 2: Attach Color B in any dc, ch 3, 4 dc in same st, *hdc in next st, sc in next st, hdc in next st, 5 dc in fourth st (Figure 2); repeat from * once more, complete last side of triangle, sl st to third ch of ch-3. Fasten off.

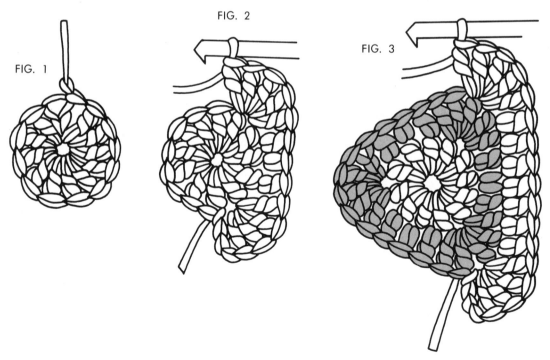

FIG. 1

FIG. 2

FIG. 3

Round 3: Attach Color C in third dc of any 5-dc corner, ch 3, 4 dc in same st, *hdc in each of next 7 sts, 5 dc in eighth st (Figure 3); repeat from * around. Sl st to third ch of ch-3. Fasten off.

Round 4: Attach Color D in middle dc of any 5-dc corner, ch 1, (2 sc, ch 1, 2 sc) in same st, *sc in every st till next corner's middle dc st, (2 sc, ch 1, 2 sc) in that st (Figure 4); repeat from * around. Sl st to first sc made. Fasten off.

FIG. 4

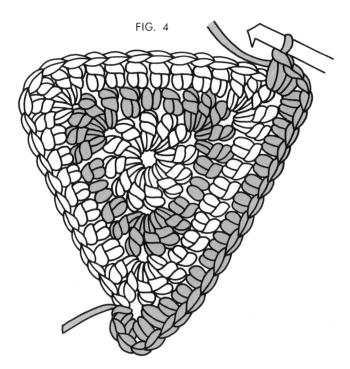

Graphic Granny Six (See Child's Afghan, Color Plate 3)

Row 1: Ch 4, 2 dc in fourth ch from hook, ch 5 (Figure 1). Turn.

Row 2: 2 dc in fourth ch from hook, ch 1, 3 dc in third ch of ch-3, ch 5 (Figure 2). Turn.

Row 3: 2 dc in fourth ch from hook, ch 1, 3 dc in ch-1 sp, ch 1, 3 dc in third ch of ch-3, ch 5 (Figure 3). Turn.

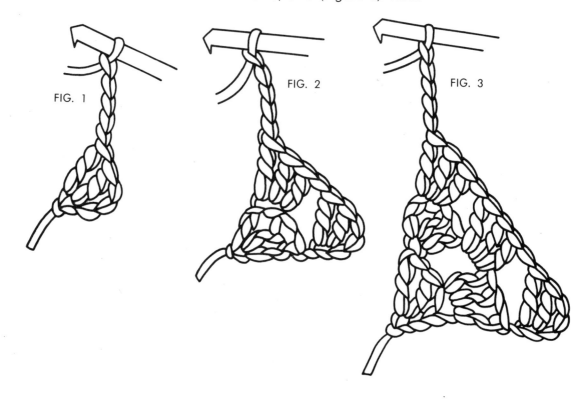

FIG. 1   FIG. 2   FIG. 3

Row 4: 2 dc in fourth ch from hook, (ch 1, 3 dc) in each ch-1 sp across, ch 1, 3 dc in third ch of ch-3, ch 5 (Figure 4). Turn.

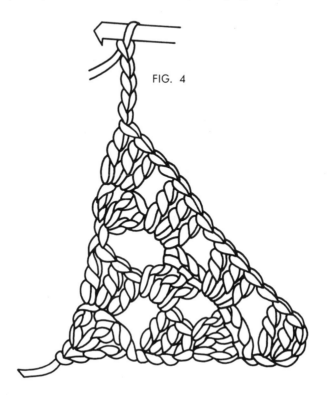

FIG. 4

Repeat Row 4 for pattern, making as many rows as desired. Make 3 more quarter granny motifs, each of a different color, and each having the same number of rows. Sew them together to form a square. If desired, work single crochet edging all around with a fifth color.

Graphic Granny Seven *(See Afghan, Color Plate 3)*

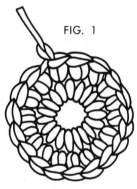

FIG. 1

Round 1: In Color A, ch 6, sl st in first ch to form ring, ch 1, work 9 sc in ring, sl st in first sc.

Round 2: Ch 1, work 2 sc in each sc around, sl st in first sc (18 sc). Fasten off. (Figure 1)

For Section 1, crochet the following rows.

Row 1: Attach Color B in any sc, sc in same st, sc in each of next 2 sc, ch 1, turn. (3 sc)

Row 2: Sc in each sc across. Ch 1, turn. (3 sc)

Row 3: 2 sc in first sc, sc across, 2 sc in last sc. Ch 1, turn. (5 sc)

Row 4: Repeat Row 2. (5 sc)

Row 5: Repeat Row 3. (7 sc)

Row 6: Repeat Row 2. (7 sc)

Row 7: Repeat Row 3 (9 sc). Fasten off, leaving enough yarn (about 9") to sew a seam along one edge. (Figure 2)

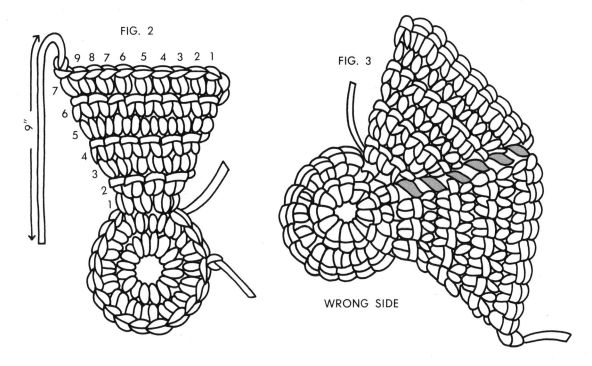

FIG. 2

FIG. 3

WRONG SIDE

For sections 2 through 6, always attach successive color in next sc on center circle. Work Rows 1–7 of Section 1 in colors C,D,E,F, and G. On wrong side sew all seams between sections together, using the 9" ends of yarn. (Figure 3)

For edging, attach Color A on right side in any sc of any section. Sc in same st and every sc till seam, *ch 1 over seam, sc in every sc of next section to seam (Figure 4); repeat from * around. Sl st to first sc. Fasten off.

FIG. 4

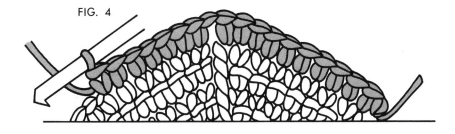

Graphic Granny Eight (See Afghan, Color Plate 3)

HOW TO DO DOUBLE SINGLE CROCHET STITCH (dsc):

Pull up loop in next st or ch (Figure 1), yo and through 1 loop on hook (Figure 2), yo and through remaining 2 loops on hook (Figure 3).

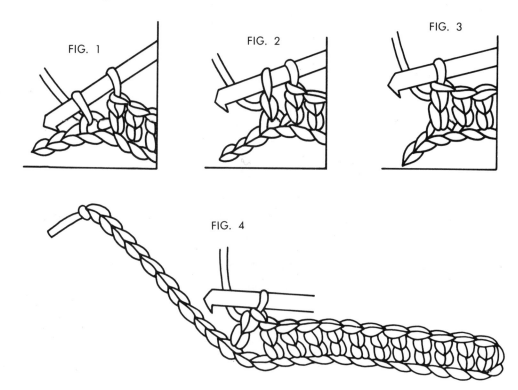

FIG. 1   FIG. 2   FIG. 3

FIG. 4

Row 1: In Color A, ch 25 loosely, dsc in second ch from hook and in next 10 ch, sk 2 ch, dsc in next ch (Figure 4) and in next 10 ch. Ch 1, turn.

Row 2: Dsc in first 10 sts, sk 2 sts, dsc in last 10 sts (Figure 5). Fasten off. Turn.

Row 3: Attach Color B in first st, ch 1, dsc in first st and in next 8 sts, sk 2 sts, dsc in last 9 sts. Ch 1, turn.

Row 4: Dsc in first 8 sts, sk 2 sts, dsc in last 8 sts. Fasten off.

Row 5: Attach Color C in first st, ch 1, dsc in first st and in next 6 sts, sk 2 sts, dsc in last 7 sts. Ch 1, turn.

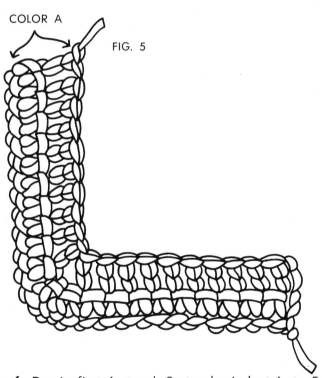

COLOR A

FIG. 5

Row 6: Dsc in first 6 sts, sk 2 sts, dsc in last 6 sts. Fasten off.

Row 7: Attach Color D in first st, ch 1, dsc in first st and in next 4 sts, sk 2 sts, dsc in last 5 sts. Ch 1, turn.

Row 8: Dsc in first 4 sts, sk 2 sts, dsc in last 4 sts. Fasten off.

Row 9: Attach Color E in first st, ch 1, dsc in first st and in next 2 sts, sk 2 sts, dsc in last 3 sts. Ch 1, turn.

Row 10: Dsc in first 2 sts, sk 2 sts, dsc in last 2 sts. Ch 1, turn.

Row 11: Dsc in first st, sk 2 sts, dsc in last st. Fasten off. (Figure 6)

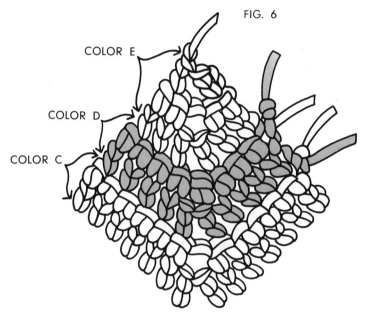

FIG. 6

COLOR E

COLOR D

COLOR C

5

Strip Patchwork

One major advantage of patchwork crochet is that it allows you to work on a very large project a small piece at a time. Imagine crocheting a queen-size bedspread or large afghan in a continuous row-by-row pattern. You would have to handle a very weighty project and would not be able to carry it along with you to work on wherever you go.

The ripple pattern, with its attractive zigzag effect, has long been a favorite crochet pattern for afghans. Traditionally, you would crochet it in one piece. In this chapter, it appears as a strip, having one zigzag repeat. To make an afghan, you crochet many strips and then sew them together. The result is the same charming traditional ripple pattern. If the afghan appears too narrow, you can crochet more strips and attach them to the sides of the afghan. All the other strip patterns can also be utilized for afghans, as well as pillows, rugs, bedspreads, planters, garments, and shawls.

Each strip can be started and then crocheted to as long a piece as desired. Strips can be used in groups of individual strips hanging together side by side for room dividers and curtains. Or, they can be sewn together to form an all-over pattern. Though the pattern will not have the same look as a group of granny squares sewn together, it will have an elegant linear or striped effect of some early patchwork designs.

The strips can be executed in any number of materials, from worsted-weight and rug yarn to novelty yarns such as straw, rope, and metallics. Though some strips, as Strip Two and Strip Three, display their intricate texture most effectively when crocheted in a solid color, each of the others looks best when it is worked in a pleasing combination of a few colors.

Strip One (See *Pillow, Color Plate 2*)

Chain 22.

Row 1: Sc in second ch from hook and in next 9 chains, 3 sc in next ch, sc in each of next 10 ch (Figure 1). Ch 1, turn piece.

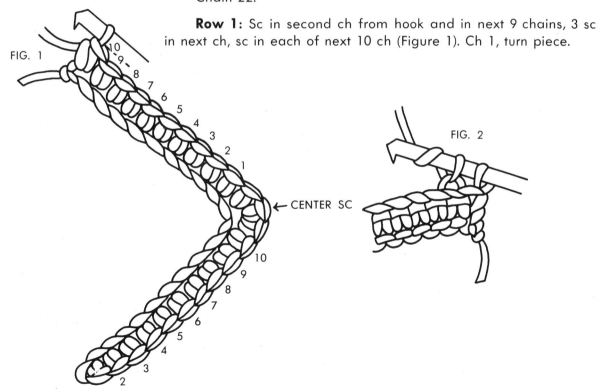

Row 2: Skip first sc; *working only into the back loops of each stitch from now on,* sc in next sc (Figure 2), sc in each of next 9 sc,

3 sc in point sc (center sc of 3-sc group), sc in each of next 10 sc, do not work in last sc (Figure 3). Ch 1, turn piece.

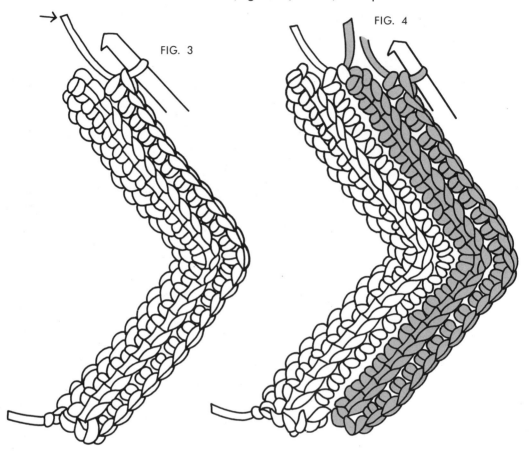

FIG. 3

FIG. 4

Repeat Row 2 for ripple pattern. Working into the back loops of the stitches will result in a ridge texture. Change colors every 2 rows, 4 rows, or wherever desired. (Figure 4)

To change colors at end of the row, ch 1 in the new color. Fasten off the odd color.

To attach strips together, make desired number of strips identical in length and with the same number of rows. Sew them together, matching the ridges across.

Strip Two *(See Afghan, Color Plate 6)*

Row 1: Ch 6, sl st in first ch to form ring, ch 3, 8 sc into ring (Figure 1), ch 4. Turn to wrong side.

Row 2: In second dc, work dc, *ch 1, dc in next dc; repeat from * 6 times, working last dc in third ch of ch-3 (Figure 2). Turn.

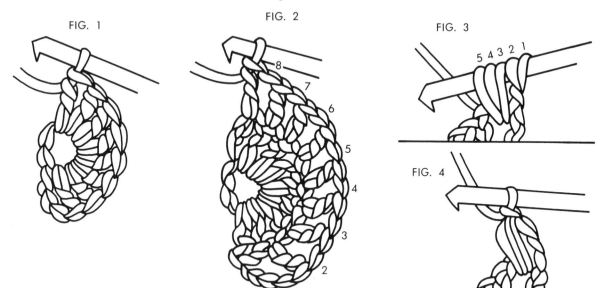

FIG. 1

FIG. 2

FIG. 3

FIG. 4

Row 3: Sl st into first sp, pull up loop on hook to ½", *(yo, pull up ½" loop in sp) twice (Figure 3), yo and through all loops on hook, ch 1 tightly to fasten st (puff st made) (Figure 4); make another puff st in same sp, then make 2 puff sts in each of next 3 sps, ch 4, make 2 puff sts in each of next 4 sps. Turn. (Figure 5)

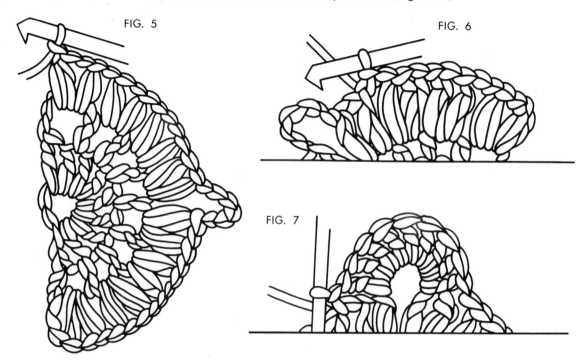

FIG. 5

FIG. 6

FIG. 7

Row 4: (Sl st after puff st, ch 1) 6 times till 2 puff sts away from ch-4 sp (Figure 6), work 9 dc sts in ch-4 sp, sl st in sp 2 puff sts away from center hole on other side (Figure 7). Turn.

Row 5: Sl st in first dc, ch 4, dc in next dc, *ch 1, dc in next dc; repeat from *6 times, having 8 spaces (Figure 8). Turn.

Repeat Rows 3 to 5 for pattern.

To complete top of strip, work a Row 4 of pattern, but do not ch 4 in center of shell.

For edging, proceed as follows.

Row 1: Attach Color B in sp after first puff st of top or bottom shell, sc in same sp, ch 1, sc in sp after next puff st, *ch 5, sc in sp after first puff st on next shell, ch 1, sc in sp after next puff st; repeat from * across length of strip (Figure 9), ch 1, turn.

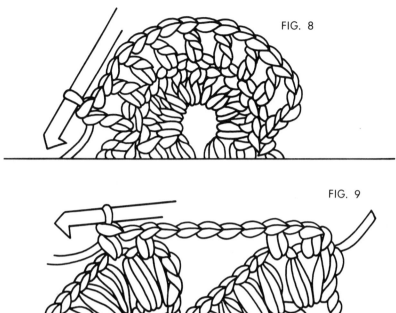

FIG. 8

FIG. 9

Row 2: Sc in first sc, sc in ch-1 sp, sc in sc, *sc in each of the 5 ch, sc in sc, sc in ch-1 sp, sc in sc; repeat from * across. Fasten off. Work same edging on other side of strip.

Strip Three

Chain 14 *very loosely.*

Row 1: In fourth ch from hook, work (dc, ch 2, 2 dc), ch 4, skip 4 ch, sl st in next ch (Figure 1), ch 2, turn piece to wrong side, work dc in each of next 3 ch (Figure 2), ch 2, turn piece again, work dc in first dc and next 2 dc; ch 1, skip 4 ch, (2 dc, ch 2, 2 dc) in last ch (Figure 3). Turn.

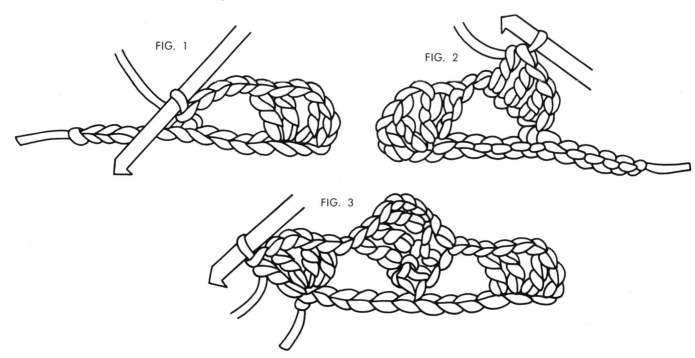

Row 2: Sl st in second dc and into ch-2 sp, (ch 3, dc, ch 2, 2 dc) in same sp, ch 8 (2 dc, ch 2, 2 dc) in shell on other side. Turn.

Rows 3 and 4: Repeat Row 2.

Row 5: Sl st in second dc and into ch-2 sp, (ch 3, dc, ch 2, 2 dc) in same sp, ch 4, sc very *loosely* into top loop of diamond, working over the 3 ch strings, ch 2 (Figure 4), turn piece to wrong side, work dc in each of next 3 ch, ch 2, turn piece again, work dc in first dc and next 2 dc, ch 1, (2 dc, ch 2, 2 dc) into shell on other side.

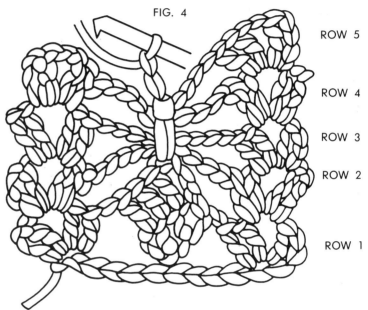

FIG. 4

ROW 5

ROW 4

ROW 3

ROW 2

ROW 1

Repeat Rows 2 to 5 for pattern.

To finish top of panel, complete a Row 5 of pattern.

For last row, work shell in first shell, ch 4, sl st in top of diamond, ch 4, work shell in last shell. Fasten off.

For edging, attach Color B into first dc st on long side of strip, work 2 sc sts into same sp, then 2 sc sts into every dc st on edge. Ch 1, turn. Work another row of sc.

Strip Four

For flower motif, proceed as follows.

In Color A, ch 5, sl st in first ch to form ring, ch 1, *sc in ring, ch 6, sc in second ch from hook, hdc in next 4 ch (Figure 1), sc in ring, ch 4, sc in second ch from hook, hdc in next 2 ch (Figure 2); repeat from * 3 more times, forming 8 petals. Sl st in first sc made. Fasten off. (Figure 3)

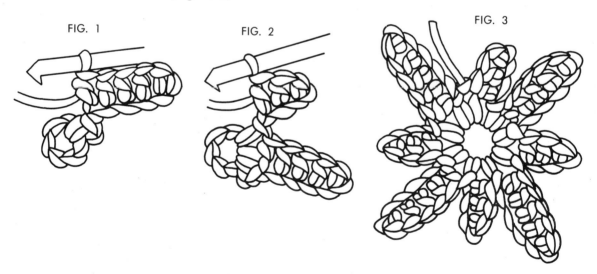

FIG. 1   FIG. 2   FIG. 3

To sew flowers together, sew small petal of first flower to small petal of second flower, skip 3 petals on second flower, sew fourth petal to small petal of third flower. Continue in this manner.

For edging on both sides of the flower strip, proceed as follows.

Row 1: Attach Color B into top sc on first petal of first flower on strip, ch 1, sc in same st, *ch 4, sc in top of second petal, ch 4, sc in top of third petal, then sc in first petal of next flower; repeat from * across length of strip (Figure 4). Ch 2, turn.

FIG. 4

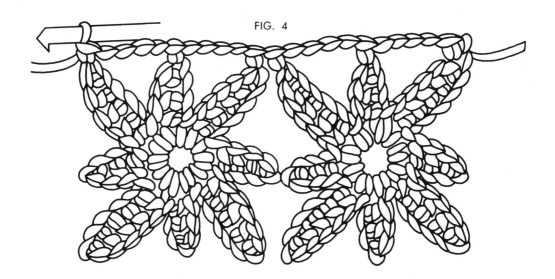

Row 2: Dc in first sc, *4 dc in ch-4 sp, dc in next sc, 4 dc in ch-4 sp, dc in each of next 2 sc; repeat from * across, ending with dc in last sc. Fasten off.

Strip Five (See Afghan, Color Plate 7)

FIRST STAR MOTIF

Round 1: In Color A, ch 6, sl st in first ch to form ring, ch 4, keeping last loop of each of the following sts on hook, work 3 trc in ring (Figure 1), yo and through all loops on hook, ch 1 tightly to fasten st, ch 3, *keeping last loop of each of the following sts on hook, work 4 trc in ring, yo and through all 5 loops on hook, ch 1 tightly, ch 3; repeat from * 4 more times. Sl st to top of first star point. Fasten off. (Figure 2)

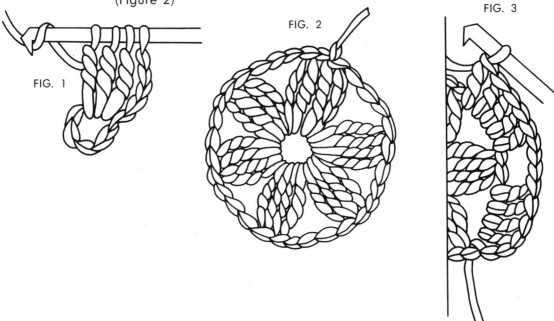

FIG. 1

FIG. 2

FIG. 3

Round 2: Attach Color B in any ch-3 sp, ch 3, 4 dc in same sp, *ch 3, 5 dc in next sp (Figure 3); repeat from * 4 times, ch 3, sl st to third ch of ch-3. Fasten off.

SECOND STAR MOTIF

Round 1: Repeat Round 1 of First Star Motif.

Round 2: Attach Color B in any ch-3 sp, ch 3, 4 dc in same sp, ch 1, holding first motif alongside second motif, sl st in any ch-3 sp of first motif, ch 1, 5 dc in next ch-3 sp of second motif, ch 1, sl st in next ch-3 sp of first motif (Figure 4), ch 1; complete second motif as for first motif. Fasten off. Make and attach as many star motifs as desired.

FIG. 4

For edging, proceed as follows.

Row 1: On right side, attach Color C in any ch-3 sp after top 5-dc cluster on one short side of strip. Working on long side, ch 7, *sc in back loop of third dc of 5-dc group, ch 3, sc in ch-3 sp, ch 3, sc in back loop of third dc of 5-dc group, ch 3, 2 trc in sp between 2 motifs, ch 3; repeat from * across length of strip. End with trc in last sp (Figure 5). Ch 1, turn.

FIG. 5

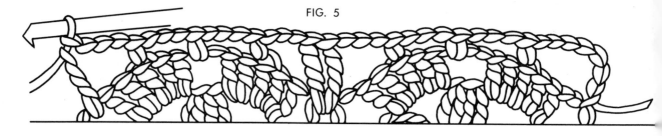

Row 2: Sc in trc, *(ch 3, sc in sc) 3 times, ch 3, sc in each of next 2 trc; repeat from * across, ending with sc in fourth ch of previous row's ch-7 (Figure 6). Ch 1, turn.

FIG. 6

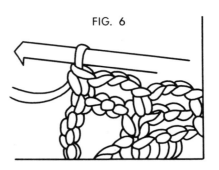

Row 3: Sc in first sc, *(ch 3, sc in sc) 3 times, ch 3, sc in each of next 2 sc; repeat from * to end, working 1 sc in last sc. Ch 1, turn.

Repeat Row 3 for stripe pattern, working as many rows as desired.

Work same on other side of strip.

Strip Six *(See Afghan, Color Plate 2)*

Pattern is a multiple of 6 + 2. For each medallion, chain 6, then chain an extra 2 chs.

For practice purposes, ch 14 *loosely* in Color A.

Row 1: Sc in second ch from hook, *skip 2 ch, 7 dc in next ch, skip 2 ch, sc in next ch; repeat from * across, ending with sc in last ch (Figure 1). Fasten off.

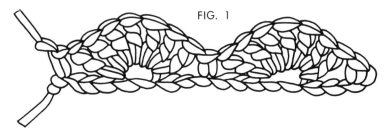

FIG. 1

Attach Color A on other side of chaining row in last sc made, sc in same sp, and repeat from * of Row 1 to complete the medallion pattern (Figure 2). Fasten off.

FIG. 2

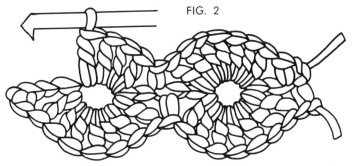

Row 2: On right side of work, attach Color B in first sc of last row worked, ch 4, *work 1 dc, 1 hdc, 1 sc, skip 1 st, then 1 sc, 1 hdc, 1 dc, 1 trc into sc (Figure 3); repeat from * across. Fasten off. Turn.

FIG. 3

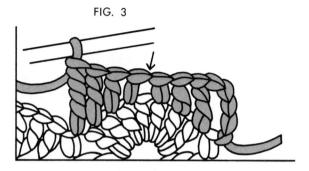

Row 3: Attach Color C in first st, ch 1, sc in same st, *working *very loosely*, pull up loop in next 2 sts (Figure 4), yo and through all 3 loops on hook (Figure 5); repeat from * across, ending with sc in fourth ch of ch-4. Fasten off. Turn. (Piece will be puckered after this round.)

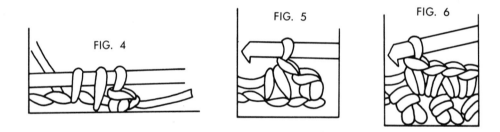

FIG. 4   FIG. 5   FIG. 6

Row 4: Attach Color B in first sc, ch 1, sc in same st, * 2 sc in next st (Figure 6); repeat from * across, ending with sc in last sc. Fasten off. Repeat Rows 2–4 on other side of medallions.

6

The Newfangled Patchwork Crochet Techniques

Crocheting is one of the most versatile crafts. The effects you can create with it are endless and varied. This chapter will serve to stretch your imagination, to open you up to the ways in which you could experiment with materials, textures, and shapes in order to create unusual, original patchwork crochet items for you and your home.

Calico Crochet

When we think of traditional fabric patchwork, we think of scraps of different prints, usually bright, miniflowered calicos, that are sewn together to form patterns. In crocheting, you could also achieve the quaint, colorful look of a conglomeration of prints. Naturally, the main ingredient in calico prints is the abundance of colors. Therefore, to capture a calico look, you have to use a variety of colors. Small amounts of yarn left over from other crochet projects can be utilized for crocheting calico patterns, making this technique ideal for a leftover or recycled yarns.

The following two calico patterns have been designed to form the same size square, provided they are all crocheted with the same weight yarn. For each separate square you crochet, choose a combination of at least three different colors. For instance, one square of Calico Pattern One can be done in red, white, and blue. Another square of the same pattern can be blue, yellow, and green. Continue creating squares in this manner, using both calico patterns, and make a multitude of squares each unique in coloration. Follow the instructions given in Chapter I for weaving ends through the back of the work to fasten all strands of yarn which hang on either side of the squares. Then arrange the motifs side by side for the most effective calico look. Each motif is a square made up of rows running horizontally forming a striped effect. You can arrange the squares with the stripes running horizontally, vertically, or in alternate directions to form all sorts of striped and broken-stripe pattern variations.

This technique can be utilized to create charming household items, especially for homes with a country or Early-American decor. Some possibilities are bedspreads, pillows, potholders, afghans, placemats (made of straw yarn), and rugs.

Calico Pattern One (See Pillow, Color Plate 7)

Note: Do not turn piece at the end of each row, but work all rows on right side of work.

Chain 20 in Color A.

Row 1: Dc in fourth ch from hook (Figure 1); dc in next ch and every ch across. Fasten off. (17 dc sts + a ch-3 at beginning) (Figure 2)

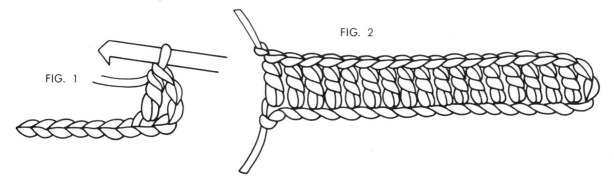

FIG. 1

FIG. 2

Row 2: Attach Color B in third ch of ch-3 of Row 1; ch 3, dc in next dc, *ch 2, skip 2 dc, dc in each of next 2 dc; repeat from * across. Fasten off. (Figure 3)

FIG. 3

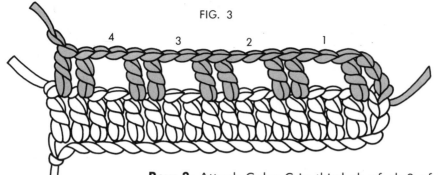

Row 3: Attach Color C in third ch of ch-3 of Row 2; ch 1, sc in same sp, sc in next dc, *dc *loosely* in each of next 2 skipped dc on Row 1 (Figure 4), sc in each of next 2 dc; repeat from * across. Fasten off. (Figure 5)

FIG. 4

FIG. 5

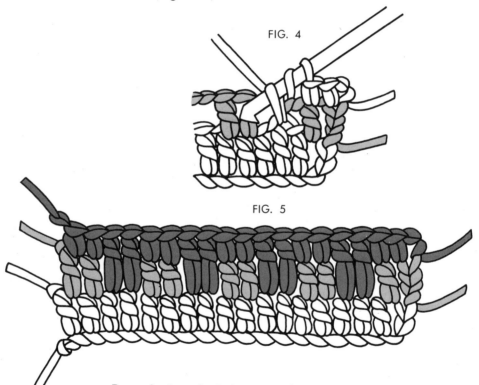

Row 4: Attach Color A in first sc of Row 3, ch 3, dc in next st and every st across. Fasten off.

Repeat Rows 2–4 for pattern and work till a square is formed.

Calico Pattern Two (See Pillow, Color Plate 7)

Note: Do not turn piece at the end of each row, but work all rows on right side of work.

Chain 19 in Color A.

Row 1: Dc in fourth ch from hook, *ch 1, skip 1 ch, dc in each of next 2 ch; repeat from * across. (Figure 1)

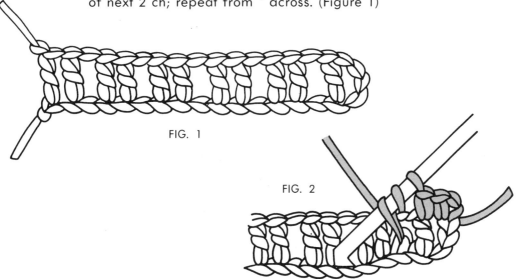

FIG. 1

FIG. 2

Row 2: Attach Color B in third ch of ch-3 of Row 1, ch 1, sc in same sp and in next dc, *dc *loosely* into skipped ch below (Figure 2), sc in next 2 dc; repeat from * across. Fasten off. (Figure 3)

FIG. 3

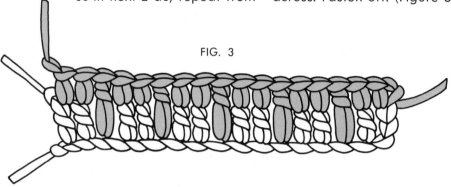

Row 3: Attach Color C in first sc of Row 2, ch 3, dc in next sc, *ch 1, skip 1 st, dc in each of next 2 sts; repeat from * across. Fasten off.

Row 4: Attach Color B in third ch of ch-3 of Row 3, ch 1, sc in same sp, sc in next dc, *dc *loosely* into skipped st below, sc in next 2 dc; repeat from * across. Fasten off.

Repeat Rows 3 and 4 till a square is formed.

Mixed Media Patchwork Crochet

One of the best ways to introduce variety and a new look to a crochet project is to use unconventional materials. Such novelty yarns as raffia, rope, metallics, and fine, pliable wire can achieve striking effects. Naturally, you would not make an afghan or a sweater from straw or wire, but imagine a room-divider, lampshade, or basket crocheted from these offbeat materials.

You could experiment with materials even further. Imagine taking small geometric pieces of wood, leather, plastic, or fabric and treating them as patchwork crochet components. Wherever necessary, depending on the material used, holes are punched all around every piece, then crocheting is done into the edge of each of the pieces. The crocheting serves not only as an unusual embellishment, but also enables you to sew such materials as wood, plastic, and leather together.

The following is an exploration of these unconventional mixed media patchwork crochet techniques.

CROCHETING INTO LEATHER AND SUEDE

Cut pieces of leather or suede to specific sizes or work with small odd-shaped scraps. For punching holes into the edges, use a rotary hole puncher. Especially designed for leathercraft, it is available in most craft stores (Figure 1). Adjust the hole puncher for the size hole required. This depends on how thick the yarn and how big the hook.

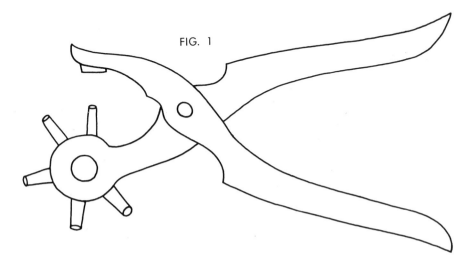

FIG. 1

Upper left: *Shoulder bag by Lissi Sigillo. Made of denim scraps and crocheting with beads.* Top center: *Shoulder bag by Ann Anderson. Made of suede, beads, branches, and macrame.* Right: *Pillow cover by Laura Holtorf. Made of crocheted squares and crochet appliqued on squares of fabric.* Bottom: *Afghan by Randie Moskowitz. Made of squares of felt, fur, and cotton prints crocheted into with solid and multicolored yarn.*

Punch holes around the pieces, distributing them evenly and being careful to make a hole at each corner. Attach yarn in any side hole, single crochet in same space, chain 1, single crochet in next hole, chain 1. Work in this manner till the corner. In the corner hole, work a single crochet, chain 2, single crochet (Figure 2). Complete other sides of piece, working all the corners the same way. Work a slip stitch into first single crochet made in order to join the round. Fasten off yarn. If desired, make a second round, working single crochet in every single crochet stitch and every chain-1 space. In each corner space, work three single crochet stitches.

Sew the pieces together as with granny squares for pillows, handbags, tote bags, purse accessories, or even wallhangings. For more variety, each geometric shape could be leather-tooled or painted with leather dyes prior to edging with crochet.

FIG. 2

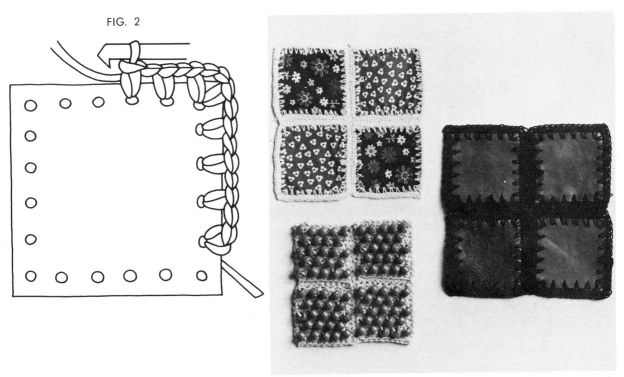

Top left: *Crocheting into Fabric* Bottom left: *Crocheting with Beads* Right: *Crocheting into Leather*

CROCHETING INTO FUR

Small scraps of rabbit, fox, muskrat, and other furs can be combined in the patchwork manner to create warm, cozy afghans and other interesting items.

If the fur is tough, punch holes around the pieces. In most cases, it will be soft and pliable and holes can be punched as you crochet the first round. Work into the edges with a sharp steel crochet hook. The second round could be done with a larger aluminum hook.

CROCHETING INTO FABRIC

From your collection of scraps from sewing projects, choose left-overs of woolens, flannels, linenlike fabrics, cottons and denims. Cut pieces into desired shapes—squares, strips, circles. Though recommended for neatness, in most cases it will not be necessary to hem the edges of these pieces since the crocheted edge will cover the cut edges. Work the same way as with fur, using a sharp crochet hook to punch and crochet all around the pieces.

This technique can be used to make afghans, pillows, kitchen curtains, and even garments. A novelty approach would be to embroider each geometric piece of solid-color fabric before adding the crocheted edging. Alternating squares of fabric with fully crocheted squares in a checkerboard pattern would also yield unusual effects.

CROCHETING INTO WOOD AND PLASTIC

Cut thin plywood or plastic, about $1/4$ inch thick, into small square or round pieces, using a jigsaw. With an electric drill, drill holes around each of the pieces, and, if desired, stain or paint the wood pieces. Then crochet around the pieces as you would into suede, using straw yarn, rope, or other novelty material. Sew the pieces together to form wall hangings, attractive room-dividers, trivets, and plant stands.

USING FABRIC AS A YARN

Purchase yard goods of cotton or cottonlike fabrics with selvages (finished edges on either side) intact. To prepare continuous $1/2$ inch strips of fabric, snip through selvage at one edge, $1/2$ inch from raw cut edge of fabric. Tear or cut fabric to within $3/8$ inch of

FIG. 3

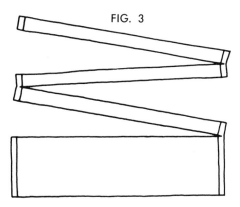

opposite selvage. Do not cut through selvage (Fig. 3). At this point, measure $\frac{1}{2}$ inch along selvage and snip again. Tear the fabric to within $\frac{3}{8}$ inch of starting selvage. Continue in this manner until all the fabric is torn. Then roll strip into a ball. Choose any motif or strip in the book and crochet it with the fabric strips, using a large crochet hook. For variety, use prints, knits, ginghams, and other unusually textured fabrics.

Single motifs, crocheted with strips of fabric, can serve as coasters, placemats, and pot holders. A few motifs sewn together can form rugs and bathroom accessories. Provided cotton, acrylic, or polyester fabrics are used for making any of these projects, the item will be machine washable.

CROCHETING INTO A RING

With a little imagination, you can apply this simple and quick technique to create charming, handcrafted gift items in a minimum of time.

The best type of ring to use is the plastic or bone ring, usually used for hanging kitchen curtains. They come in a variety of sizes, with 1 inch in diameter being the most useful for this technique, and they are available at most craft stores and department store needlework departments.

Though regular worsted-weight yarn, straw yarn, and metallic yarn can be used to crochet into these rings, the most common material for projects is mercerized crochet cotton, which can be obtained in a variety of colors. The hook used with this yarn is a Size 1 steel crochet hook.

To crochet into a ring, attach yarn to the ring the same way you would attach a second color to a motif (see page 28). Chain 1,

FIG. 4

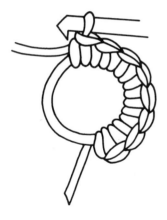

then work single crochet stitches into the ring until it is completely covered with stitches (Fig. 4). When the end of the round is reached, work a slip stitch into the first single crochet stitch made in order to join the round. Fasten off the yarn. Thread each end of yarn into a tapestry needle and weave it through the back of the single crochet stitches. Clip off the remainder. Continue in this manner, making a number of crochet-covered plastic rings. Then arrange the completed rings to form circles, squares, hexagons, triangles. With a double strand of regular sewing thread, sew adjacent rings together on the back of the work through the stitches, making sure the stitching does not show on the right side.

This very simple technique can be used to make coasters, placemats, trivets, hot pads, and other small household items. When crocheted into with metallic yarn, these rings can be sewn into unusual necklaces, bracelets, earrings, belts, and other wearable accessory items.

Besides crocheting into symmetrical shapes as rings, interesting effects can be achieved by crocheting into various asymmetrical pieces of hardware, as metal drains with punched holes, key rings, and washers. You can even improvise further by stringing beads onto the yarn before attaching it to the ring, then crocheting the beads in as you work the first round into the ring.

Left: Placemat (see *Using Fabric as Yarn*. Right: Coasters (see *Crocheting into Rings*)

CROCHETING WITH BEADS

Creating with beads is in itself a craft. Usually beads are threaded together or sewn to fabric to form decorative patterns. Beads can also be worked into a piece of crochet with unusual effects in combination with the yarn.

Beads are available in many colors, shapes, and materials. The best ones for crocheting are round, made of either wood, glass, minerals, or ceramic material.

Purchase beads with holes large enough to accommodate the thickness of the yarn. String all beads onto yarn, threading end of yarn into a tapestry needle for ease of pulling the yarn through the holes. (Figure 5)

FIG. 5

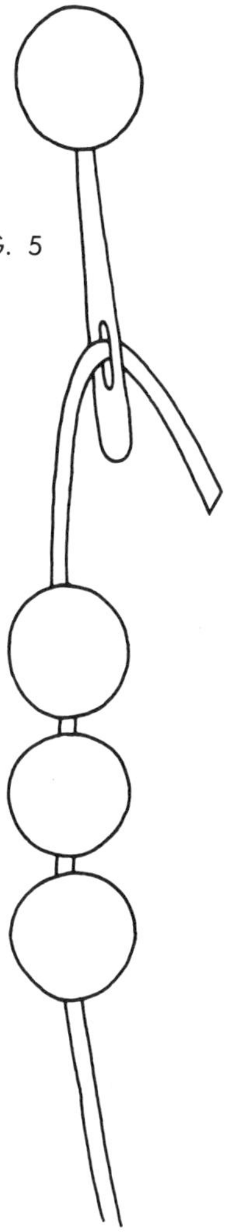

Chain as per instructions or 15 chains for practice piece.

Row 1: (right side of work) Sc in second ch from hook and every ch across. Ch 1, turn.

Row 2: (wrong side of work) Sc in first sc, *bring one bead up to work, sc in next 2 sc (Figure 6); repeat from * across. Ch 1, turn.

Row 3: (right side of work) Sc in every sc across. Ch 1, turn.

Row 4: (wrong side of work) Sc in first 2 sc, *bring one bead up to work, sc in next 2 sc; repeat from * across. Ch 1, turn.

Row 5: (right side of work) Sc in every sc across. Ch 1, turn.

Repeat Rows 2 to 5 for beaded crochet pattern and work till piece is square in shape. Fasten off.

Any granny motif that contains a single crochet round can have beads worked into it. This beaded single crochet round should be done on the wrong side of the motif so that the beads will protrude from the right side. Sew beaded squares together to form pillows and other household items. Large, solid nonpatchwork areas can be crocheted with beads to make beaded handbags. In addition, you could use this simple method to form a beaded edging on a crocheted garment when working the single crochet edging rows.

FIG. 6

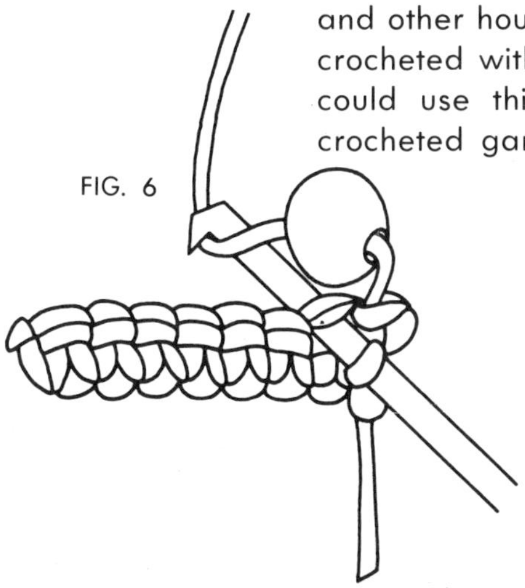

Free-Form Patchwork Crochet

It is possible to approach a patchwork crochet project much like most artists approach their empty canvasses — with some vague plan of action, but mainly with the intention to improvise and play it by ear.

With crocheting, you can sculpt and form interesting shapes without a great deal of experience in the craft. Choose any motif in this book, crochet the first one or two rounds following directions. Then take off on your own, building your motif into a weird, asymmetrical shape. Crochet a third of the next round in single crochet, the second part in double crochet, and the last third in triple crochet. Or, begin a round and work it only halfway around. Try inserting a novelty stitch or unusual stitch formation appearing in another motif or try creating your own stitches. In free form patchwork crochet, anything goes.

Keep in mind, too, that you must strive to be imaginative and unconventional in your use and arrangement of color. In free form crochet, a multitude of colors, usually not too harmonious, gives the piece an eye-catching patchwork look. (See Color Plate 8.) Try to change colors frequently, often in mid-round.

Work all the odd-shaped pieces to approximately a similar size. On a flat surface, experiment with arranging the motifs together side by side until there is a harmonious color composition, with not too much of one particular color in any one area. Attempt, too, to fit these odd-shaped pieces together with the minimum of open areas between the motifs. Pin the pieces together and, on the wrong side, sew each seam using a matching color yarn. Later, if you wish, you can fill the empty areas by crocheting little circles (see Round 1 of Graphic Granny One, page 101) and sewing one into every hole.

Though you could try to work the pieces as flat as possible from the onset, the conglomeration of stitches you use will sometimes cause the motifs to curl and not lie flat. That can be easily remedied by pressing the pieces lightly before you sew them together or later when the project is completed. Refer to instructions in Chapter I, page 42, for blocking projects.

MAKING FREE FORM PATCHWORK GARMENTS

Free form patchwork motifs can be most easily and effectively joined to form flat projects, such as wall hangings, afghans, and pillows. It is also possible to make simple garments with them, such as vests and sweaters.

The best method of constructing garments to fit is to work from a flat pattern. Purchase a commercial paper pattern, designed for knits only, for the garment you desire. Cut away all seam allowances. (Crocheted sweaters, when sewn together, do not have allowances at the seams, but are sewn edge to edge.) Trace the paper pattern onto heavy paper. As you crochet each free form motif, arrange it

Left: *Wall hanging by Martha Albert. Freeform crochet in earth tones suspended on a branch.* Right: *Wall hanging by Randie Moskowitz. Freeform crochet in various shades of solid and multicolored yarns.*

FIG. 1

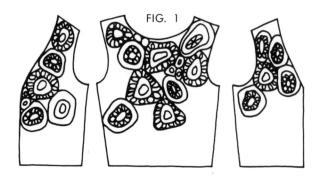

on the pattern alongside other motifs (Figure 1). Sew the pieces together periodically. Try to crochet successive motifs to fit into specific open areas till the pattern is completely filled with motifs which follow the curve and shaping of the pattern. Later, when all the major seams are sewn, work a few rows of edging around the garment to fill in and round out all the edges.

THE PATCHWORK CROCHETING BEE

Since free form patchwork does not require great expertise in crocheting, it serves as a most appropriate, exciting project for a group of people, especially a group of beginner crocheters. It is very easy to organize the "Crocheting Bee." Have each of the members supply a skein or two of yarn. Then, the yarn is distributed among the members, with each person taking a substantial amount of a number of different color yarns. The group may work together, as in a classroom or in a member's home, or each member can do the work at home. Each is required to improvise patchwork components which involve:

1. Creating a color combination with the colors available, a different combination for each motif.
2. Experimenting with unusual stitches and techniques.
3. Making the motif a feasible size, as established by the group. Symmetry should be discouraged.

When each of the members has completed a number of motifs, the group gathers to assemble them, with one person being in charge of the actual sewing and finishing. The finished product can become an afghan, wall hanging, collection of pillows, or any number of unusual items. Any of these can serve as a most charming and marketable bazaar item.

7

Patchwork Crochet Projects

Furnished with a collection of over fifty patchwork crochet techniques and motifs to select from, the fulfilling pursuit of creating with them is now yours. This is your chance to exercise artistic flair in choosing an appropriate motif, a pleasing color combination, and an interesting yarn and, with effective workmanship, building an article that is an expression of *you*.

If you are a beginner in the craft of crochet, it may be wise, at first, to make a pillow, hat, scarf, or other small item. Later, you will undoubtedly find dozens of applications for patchwork crochet to accent your home and wardrobe. Some fascinating possibilities you may consider are:

• A room-divider, made of straw or jute yarn. Suspended from a wooden dowel, or hung by hooks from the ceiling, this panel could consist of separate strips or many motifs sewn together into an all-over pattern.

147

• A grouping of hanging planters, made of a variety of motifs and strips in rug yarn and jute twine.

• An area rug to accent a living room, hallway, or family room with large floor cushions to match.

• Bathroom accessories which could include a bathroom seat cover, a floor mat, tissue box and spray can covers, and possibly shower curtains (with a plastic liner).

• A lampshade for a lamp suspended over a dining area, made of straw or cotton yarn. This should be loosely worked, to allow light to shine through. A matching tablecloth or placemats will complete the decor beautifully.

• A fitted bedspread on a day bed or a slipcover for a simple chair or sofa. Throw pillows, done in a variety of motifs but in the same color combination as the slipcover, will be charming additions.

• Interior decorations for an automobile, such as car seat covers and hanging accessories.

• Christmas tree ornaments, consisting of single motifs made of straw, crochet cotton, or metallics.

• A group of squares sewn together into a strip, to be attached as a trim panel to the hem of a ready-to-wear dress or a garment you make yourself. Crocheted components can also be used as trim insertion on the yoke of a blouse, down the sleeves, or on the collar to give the garment a handcrafted look.

• Fashion accessories, such as belts, bracelets, and necklaces, made of novelty yarns, as well as hats, scarves, shoulder bags, and totes.

Designing with Patchwork Crochet

Unlike other crafts which depend heavily on a proper design composition and balance of colors for effectiveness, patchwork crochet is generally successful in any way it is worked. An improvised piece containing twenty-five colors and a variety of yarn textures can have just as much charm and appeal as a three-color piece meticulously planned for dramatic color and design effect. Consequently, you can work your project in either of two ways:

you can either build your design, improvising color and shape arrangement as you crochet it, or you can design your project before you start it.

For the improvisational technique, gather whatever yarn you have available, especially leftovers from other projects. Crochet each individual motif, choosing the colors as you go along. If you are using a great many colors and textures of yarn, try to use one basic shade to pull the other colors together, either by edging each motif with it or simply by using it in greater concentration than any of the other shades. This color could be your favorite color or a basic like white, black, or brown. As you complete a number of motifs, arrange them alongside each other and, with a critical eye, determine whether the color choice and arrangement is effective. Consider, too, the end purpose of the item. If it is to be a decorative piece for the home, will it blend or clash with its surrounding decor? If it is to be a garment or wearable accessory, will it complement the clothes it will be worn with? If necessary, do not hesitate to pull out rounds of work done in unharmonious colors and either rearrange their placement or eliminate them altogether. Provided you adjust your design accordingly as you work, the piece you will create in this spontaneous manner will undoubtedly have a one-of-a-kind, handcrafted look like your grandmother's granny square afghan or her silk and satin crazy quilt.

Choosing to design your project before you start will require more planning and awareness of the principles of design and color. The process of designing is by no means mysterious or difficult. Very simply, after you decide which motif you will use and the article you want to create, you will have to select colors and plan the most pleasing arrangement of these colors.

People often wonder where the artist and designer obtain their inspiration. Ideas for form and color are all around us—in fabrics, in wallpapers, in graphic magazine advertisements, and in nature. For inspirational reference, start collecting clips from magazines which represent interesting color use and design. Be observant as the seasons change. Each time of year nature is teeming with beautiful, harmonious color ideas—the rich wines and earth tones in the autumn, the dull, opaque chocolate and green shades in the winter, the verdant garden brights in the spring, and the sunny citrus colors in the summer. Becoming aware of and structuring your design around the interesting form and color in your surroundings is the first step in learning design.

As you plan your project, experimentation should be your

rule. Making crocheted sample motifs is a very necessary step before you begin each project. Try working one motif in a variety of color combinations. Then work the same motif in one color combination, arranging the colors differently on each piece. The following illustrations show how a distinctive effect is created in each motif with each unique scheme of color arrangement (Fig. 1).

A

B

C

D

FIG. 1

Experiment with texture too by trying the unconventional. Combine unusual yarns in one motif, as cotton string and mohair, or worsted-weight and straw yarn. A fascinating study in texture would be a piece consisting of multiples of one .basic patchwork motif, with each component done in various textures of yarn — boucle, crepe, sport-weight, metallic, ombre, and cotton string. Try crocheting a motif with two strands held together as one, possibly a metallic yarn and a wool sport yarn. That would result in a dramatic, elegant look for eveningwear. Again, keep in mind the end purpose of the project. The weight and texture of the piece are important factors to consider. A garment should not be weighty and stiff, but rather soft and comfortable. A project like a tote bag should be tightly worked so it can retain its shape.

Once you arrive at an effective color combination and arrangement of motifs, make a working sketch, if possible with colored pens or pencils. Trace the geometric pattern arrangement appearing on page 154–156 that applies to the motif you are using, either square, hexagonal, or octagonal. Indicate how the motifs will be placed in terms of varying color and texture, and make a notation of how many pieces of each kind of motif you will need. Later, when you are done sewing the pieces together, you can determine which kind of edge embellishment would be most effective. Your choices are many — single crochet edging, picots, shells, yarn fringe, crocheted fringe, or beaded edging.

The inspirational material for designing in patchwork crochet available to you, both within this book and all around you, is vast. No doubt you will be able to spend many hours of pleasurable creativity in this absorbing, limitless craft.

Color

Color is perhaps the most fascinating element in patchwork crochet. It is an emotional experience and color choice is intuitive. It is a good idea to choose colors that are your favorites and that you will enjoy working with.

To help you choose colors more effectively there are a few guidelines to keep in mind.

Every color has a position on the color wheel (Fig. 2). Red, yellow, and blue are the primary colors. By combining equal parts of any two primary colors you get secondary colors — orange, green,

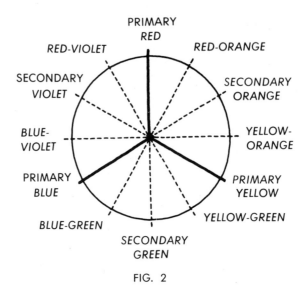

FIG. 2

and violet. Tertiary colors are adjacent to the secondary and primary colors on the wheel. Colors which lie directly across from each other are *complementary colors*. If a pair of them are placed side by side, the two complement each other, each making the other more lively and bright.

Every color on the wheel has different gradations, or values, of lightness or darkness. If white is added to a color, it becomes lighter; adding black results in a darker value.

A color scheme of two complements is called a complementary color scheme. When several colors adjacent on the wheel are combined, as red, red-orange, and orange, the color scheme is analogous. If various values of one color are combined, such as light, medium, and dark shades of red, you get a monochromatic color scheme. Each of these three types of color combinations creates a harmonious effect.

Colors are effective carriers of emotion and feeling. They can be relaxing or invigorating, cool or warm, melancholy or gay. Cool colors are those which have blue or green in them, warm colors are those which have some red or yellow. This is especially important to remember when you are trying to capture a mood in home decor with crocheted bedspreads, afghans, wall hangings, rugs and decorative accessories.

In choosing yarn you will find that there is a vast array of colors, basic ones and current fashion and decorator shades. Most yarn manufacturers prepare their yarn lines to include all the primary and secondary colors, most tertiary colors, as well as black, grey, white, and other neutrals. Yarn lines are designed to allow the greatest number of possibilities for complementary, analogous, and monochromatic color schemes.

In combining a few colors, it is important to also remember that colors, on their own, may appear to the eye in a certain way. When placed next to each other, their individual values and intensities react and may give the eye a totally different impression. Sometimes a beautiful, intense color will be affected adversely by a certain color placed next to it. The only way to determine color effect is to make crocheted sample motifs and see the effects that result. Only through this trial and error process of experimentation with colors can you derive the right proportions and combinations and begin to train your eye to work effectively with color.

The most creative way of using color is to include it as a very major aspect of the design. By crocheting shapes in colors of contrasting values and intensities, you can build fascinating geometric patterns. The exciting designs appearing in fabric patchwork quilts, Navajo rugs, and folk art patterns as well as contemporary decorator fabrics, wallpapers, and tile floors, can be duplicated in crochet patchwork. The afghan on the dust jacket is a prime example of such color application. The design is inspired by a traditional quilt pattern, called Grandmother's Flower Garden. Containing a variety of garden-bright colors, each motif is crocheted in one solid color. By arranging the individual motifs into a clever flower pattern, a charming multicolor quilt look is achieved. This pattern appears, along with other provocative arrangements of simple geometric motifs, on the next few pages. Use them as inspiration for your afghans, rugs, pillows, bedspreads, and wall hangings.

One factor to consider when working with most of these patterns is that the simpler, less intricate patchwork crochet motifs are the best ones to use for this "designing with color" technique. The concentration should be on color rather than texture and fancy stitches. Such easy-to-do motifs as Granny Square One, Two, and Three; Hexagon Granny One; and Graphic Grannies Two, Five, and Six are perfect for such application. Try to work the rounds of each individual motif in one solid color or choose a selection of monochromatic colors for each motif in the piece. For instance, work one square in shades of yellow and make its adjoining, contrasting square in shades of brown.

Once you learn to utilize color effectively, each of the motifs in the book will hold dozens of possibilities for arrangement, each pattern creating a different overall effect.

BASIC PATTERN ARRANGEMENTS OF GEOMETRIC SHAPES

SQUARES

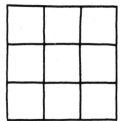

DIAMONDS (WITH SQUARES)

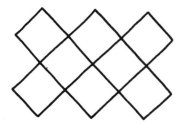

OCTAGONS

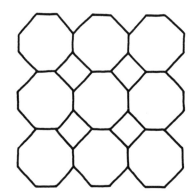

CIRCLES

HEXAGONS

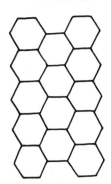

TRIANGLES

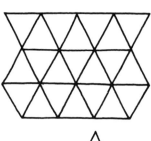

 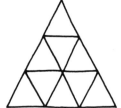

PATTERNS WITH SQUARES

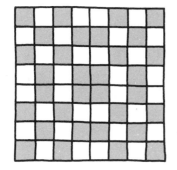
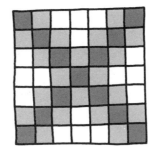
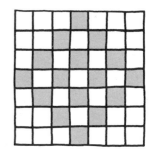

PATTERNS WITH DIAMONDS

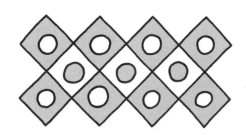
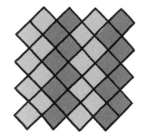
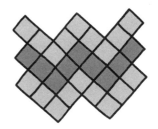

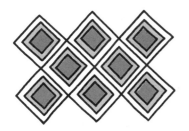
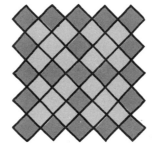

PATTERNS WITH SQUARES, HALF SQUARES AND STRIPES

PATTERNS WITH HEXAGONS

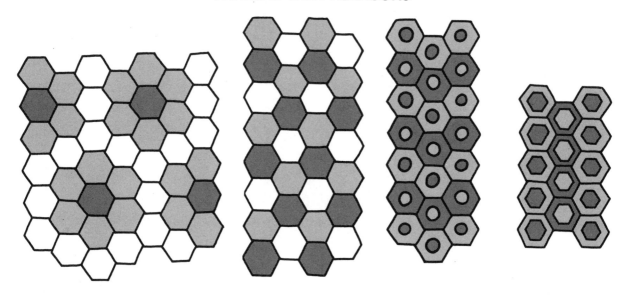

Patchwork Crochet for the Home

Afghan based on Strip Six, page 129.

Baby's afghan based on Granny Square Eight, page 59.

STANDARD AFGHAN SIZES

AFGHAN	45″ × 60″	54″ × 72″	60″ × 80″
CHILD'S AFGHAN	36″ × 48″		
BABY AFGHAN	28″ × 36″		

STANDARD BEDSPREAD SIZES

TWIN BED	81″ × 110″
DOUBLE BED	96″ × 110″
QUEEN SIZE BED	102″ × 120″
KING SIZE BED	114″ × 120″

Easy to Make Patchwork Crochet Accessories and Gifts

TOTE BAG

Purchase wooden handles with 11 inch wide horizontal slits for inserting bag portion. Or, obtain two wood dowels, $\frac{3}{8}$ inch in diameter and 12 inches in length. Then insert and glue a large round wood bead onto each of the four ends of the dowels to keep the bag portion from slipping off the dowels. Make fifteen $5\frac{1}{2}$ inch squares. Sew each group of five squares into a strip. Sew the strips together. Work two rows of double crochet on each short end of the piece. Insert each end into the slit of each handle or wrap around dowels. Fold the end over and hem it down. Sew the sides of the bag, leaving an opening of one square at the top of each side.

TISSUE BOX COVER

(Designed to fit a standard 10 inch $\times$ 5 inch $\times$ $2\frac{1}{2}$ inch tissue box) Make twenty $2\frac{1}{2}$ inch squares. Sew twelve squares into a strip. Then sew the two ends to form a tube. Make two strips of four squares each for the top of the box. Attach the two strips together by sewing only a one inch seam at each side, leaving the rest open between them so that the tissue will be able to pass through. Sew the top portion to the tube, matching all seams. Attach yarn at bottom edge of tube and work one round of double crochet, decreasing one stitch at each of the four corners. Join the round with a slip stitch. Next round: work *dc in next st, ch 1, skip 1 st; repeat from * around. Join the round and fasten off. Lace $\frac{1}{4}$ inch elastic through the holes formed by the last round. Pull elastic taut and sew both ends together. Fit the cover over the tissue box and block it lightly while it is on the box.

HANGING PLANTER FROM SQUARES

Measure around widest part of planter to determine the circumference. Divide that amount by four. Make five squares to the dimensions of a quarter of the circumference. For example, if the planter's circumference is 20 inches, a quarter of that is 5 inches, so make five 5-inch squares. Sew four squares into a strip. Attach the ends together to form a tube. Sew the fifth square into an open end. On the other edge, work single crochet or novelty edging. To

Left: Tote bag based on Granny Square One, page 45. Made of Malina's rug yarn. Top: Hanging planter based on Granny Square Two, page 48. Bottom: Tissue box cover based on Granny Square Four, page 51.

make the strings for hanging the planter, make a chain to measure approximately 40 inches. Slip stitch in every chain across. Make another string the same way. Sew each of the four ends of the two strings to a steam between two motifs. Sew the folds of the two strings together on top and hang the planter by the fold.

PLANTER MADE FROM STRIPS   (*See Color Plate 2*)

Make a strip long enough to fit around the widest part of the planter. Sew the two ends of it together to form a tube. Work a few rounds of double crochet or single crochet around one side of the tube until the tube measures the same as the height of the planter. For the bottom of the planter, make a Graphic Granny One (page 101) motif, enlarging it by working more rounds until it fills one open end of the tube. Sew the motif into the opening.

Patchwork Crochet Fashions

Patchwork crochet fashions have the same timeless, universal appeal as the well-known granny square afghan. Despite the fast-changing pace of fashion, a garment handcrafted with patchwork crochet can be fashionably almost any time. A crocheted motif or strip can be used as an appliqued adornment on a blouse or dress or the garment can be constructed completely from crocheted components.

Each item in the following group of fully-crocheted patchwork garments consists of a layout for sewing the components together and instructions for completing the item. Each of these items can be made in any one of a variety of motifs.

To begin, choose any appropriate motif in the book. Since most of the fashions are created from squares, your selection should be any granny square, square-shaped graphic granny, or fabric or leather square edged with crochet. The yarn you choose should be soft, pliable, and comfortable for any shawl, sweater, or skirt design. Such yarns as worsted-weight or sport-weight yarn, or novelties as mohair, boucle, and crepe yarn, are suitable for any of these items. Hats, scarves, and other accessories could be made of rug yarn. Refer to the size garment you are making to determine the size of the motif you will need. Make sample motifs, each in a different size hook, to arrive at the correct size motif. If every hook yields a motif that is too large, choose another motif, with fewer rounds, that will be smaller. If the motif is too small, add a round or two of single crochet all around to enlarge it. The motif should also be soft and pliant so that the garment will be comfortable to wear.

HIS AND HERS VESTS

HIS

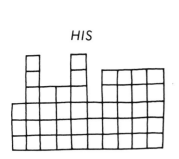

HERS

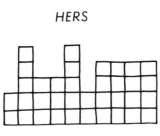

HERS

Size	Petite	Small	Medium	Large
Sweater Bust Measurement	30″	32½″	35″	37½″
Size of Square	3″ sq.	3¼″ sq.	3½″ sq.	3¾″ sq.

HIS

Size	Small 36–38	Medium 39–41	Large 42–43	X-Large 44–46
Sweater Chest Measurement	37½″	40″	42½″	45″
Size of Square	3¾″ sq.	4″ sq.	4¼″ sq.	4½″ sq.

Attach squares as in diagram.

Fold piece in half and sew into a tube. Sew shoulder seams.

Work ½ inch of single crochet edging around armholes and neckline.

For waistline ribbing, make a chain to measure 4 inches. Sc in second ch from hook and in every ch across. Ch 1, turn.

Row 2: Working only into the back loops of the stitches, sc in first sc and every sc across, forming a ridge. (See Strip One, page 117). Ch 1, turn.

Repeat Row 2 for ridge pattern.

Work till piece snugly fits the waistline. Sew last row to first row, forming a tube. Sew tube to bottom of vest.

DIAMONDS SKIRT

Size	Petite	Small	Medium	Large
Hip	34″	36″	38″	40″
Square	3¼″ sq.	3½″ sq.	3¾″ sq.	4″ sq.

Start at hip by making first tier of 8 squares and 8 triangles to size specified in chart. Work each consecutive tier down to measure ⅛ inch to ¼ inch larger per square than the previous tier. To add

⅛ inch or ¼ inch to a square, either work it in a larger hook, make a round of single crochet around each square, or make another motif that will work up larger. Sew each new tier to previous tier as you complete it. Make skirt as long as desired. Sew completed panel together into a tube.

For drawstring waistline, work single or double crochet stitches into the top of the skirt, spacing stitches so that skirt will fit around hips. At end of round, join first stitch to last stitch by working slip stitch. Continue working in rounds for about 3 inches or desired amount, decreasing a few stitches on each round so that skirt will fit loosely around waist. Make a string tie by chaining a length to measure 45 inches and working a slip stitch into every chain across. Thread the tie through one row of sc or dc stitches, between the stitches. If desired, fringe bottom of skirt to look as pictured. Block skirt to flatten all seams.

HALTER TOP

SEW TOGETHER

Size	Petite	Small	Medium	Large
Sweater Bust Measurement	30"	31½"	33"	36"
Size of Square	3½" sq. 5" diagonal	3¾" sq. 5¼" diagonal	4" sq. 5½" diagonal	4¼" sq. 6" diagonal

Make 26 squares, 7 triangles. Sew together as in diagram. Fold on dotted lines which denote side seams. Sew back seam. Work single crochet edging on bottom edge and neckline. Do novelty edging, if desired. Ties to tie halter: (Make 2) Chain a length about 18 inches long. Slip stitch in every chain across. Sew a tie to top of each square at front.

PULLOVER SWEATER

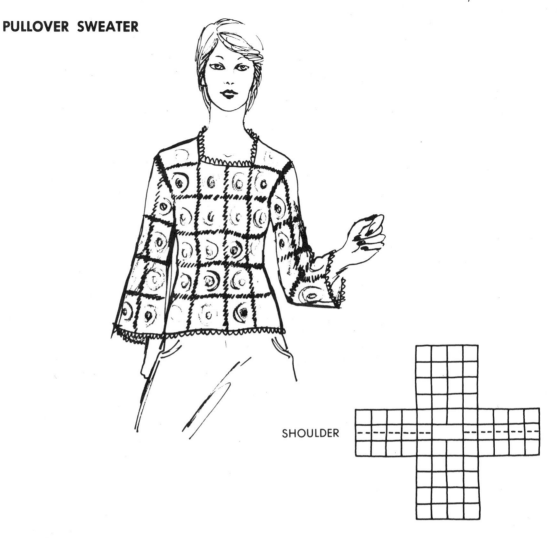

SHOULDER

Size	Small	Medium	Large	X-Large
Sweater Bust Measurement	32"	34"	36"	38"
Size of Square	4" sq.	4¹/₄" sq.	4¹/₂" sq.	4³/₄" sq.

Make 66 squares. Sew together as in diagram. Fold on dotted line (shoulder), overlap front and back, and sew the two side seams. Work single crochet edging around neckline, sleeve edges, and lower edge. If desired, make edging, such as shell or picot edge, into the single crochet rows.

PONCHO

Poncho based on Granny Square Seven, page 57. Made of Malina's Denim-Look yarn.

SEW TOGETHER

One Size Fits All

Each Square measures 5 inches square

Make 56 squares. Sew together as in diagram. Work a few rows of single crochet edging on neckline and on bottom edge. Fringe the bottom edge with 5 inch fringe, having fringes one or two stitches apart.

PULL-ON HAT

One Size Fits All

STIFF-BRIMMED HAT

See Chart For Size

PULL-ON HAT

Each square measures 5 inches square

Make 5 squares. Sew four squares together into a tube. Then sew fifth square to adjacent edges of the four squares on one side of the tube to form crown of hat. Work a few rows of single crochet edging on bottom edge of hat.

STIFF-BRIMMED HAT

NOTE: Hat is designed to be made of worsted-weight or a similar weight yarn *only.* Be sure to obtain gauge before proceeding.

Hat is made of three pieces which are sewn together — crown, brim, and patchwork crochet trim.

Size	Small	Medium
Head Size	19"–21"	22"–24"
Size of Square	3" sq.	3¼" sq.
Gauge for Crown	7 dc = 2"	7 dc = 2"

For patchwork crochet trim, make 6 squares. Sew together into a strip and then into a tube.

CROWN (Instructions for medium size appear in parenthesis.)

Round 1: Ch 4, sl st in first ch to form ring, ch 3, 11 dc in ring. Sl st to third ch of ch-3. Ch 3.

Round 2: Dc in joining st, 2 dc in next dc and every dc around. Sl st in third ch of ch-3. Ch 3. (24 dc sts)

Round 3: Dc in joining st, *dc in next 2 dc, 2 dc in third dc; repeat from * around. Sl st in third ch of ch-3. Ch 3. (32 dc sts)

Round 4: Dc in joining st, *dc in next dc, 2 dc in second dc; repeat from * around. Sl st in third ch of ch-3. Ch 3. (48 dc sts)

Round 5: Dc in joining st, *dc in next 5(3) dc, 2 dc in 6th(4th) dc; repeat from * around. Sl st in third ch of ch-3. Ch 3. [56(60) dc sts]

Round 6: Dc in joining st, *dc in next 6(4) dc, 2 dc in 7th(5th) dc; repeat from * around. Sl st in third ch of ch-3. [64(72) dc sts] Fasten off.

BRIM Working with 2 strands of yarn held together and the same size hook, ch 66(77). Being careful not to twist the chain sts, sl st in first ch to form a large ring.

Round 1: Ch 1, sc in joining and in every ch around. Sl st in first sc made.

Round 2: Ch 1, 2 sc in joining, then 2 sc in every 6th(7th) st, thereby increasing 11 sts around. Sl st to first sc made.

Round 3: Ch 1, sc in next sc and every sc around. Sl st in first sc made.

Rounds 4, 6, and 8: Increase 11 sts, evenly spaced, on each of these rounds.

Rounds 5, 7, and 9: Repeat Round 3. At the end of Round 9, fasten off.

Sew crown to top of motif tube, then sew bottom of tube to brim. Steam brim lightly.

Stiff-brimmed Hat and Cardigan Sweater based on Granny Square Three, page 49. Made of Fruit-of-the-Loom yarn.

CARDIGAN WITH SHORT OR LONG SET-IN SLEEVE

Size	Petite	Small	Medium	Large	X-Large
Sweater Bust Measurement	30"	32½"	35"	37½"	40"
Size of Square	3" sq.	3¼" sq.	3½" sq.	3¾" sq.	4" sq.

For short sleeve cardigan, make 86 squares, 6 triangles.

For long sleeve cardigan, make 116 squares, 6 triangles.

Assemble bodice and two sleeves as in diagrams. Fold each sleeve on dotted line and sew sleeve seams. Fold bodice on dotted lines and sew shoulder seams. Sew sleeves into armholes, matching seams on sleeves to seams on bodice and having seam on sleeve marked "shoulder" fall at shoulder seam. Make 3–4 rows of single crochet edging on neckline, lower edge, and edges of sleeves. If desired, make novelty edging also. For ties, make a chain to measure approximately 12 inches. Slip stitch in every chain across. Sew one tie to each top edge of cardigan, or sew a few ties down center front for a different look.

INFANT'S SWEATER, PONCHO, AND BONNET

Infant's sweater, poncho, and bonnets based on Granny Square Four, page 51.

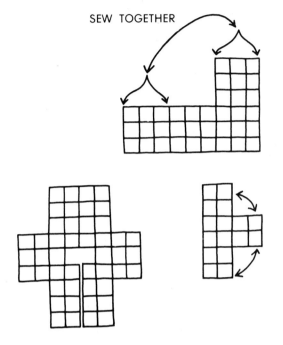

Size	6 Months	1 year	18 mos. — 2 years
Sweater Chest Measurement	20″	22″	24″
Square Size	2½″	2¾″	3″

For poncho, make 36 squares.

For sweater, make 46 squares.

For bonnet, make 16 squares.

Sew together as in diagram. Do 1 row of single crochet edging around all edges. For a second row, *work 1 single crochet, skip 1 single crochet, chain 1, single crochet in next stitch. Repeat from *, thereby making a casing through which to run all ties. On third row of edging, work a shell or picot edge. For each tie (on either bonnet, poncho, or sweater), chain a length to measure 36 inches. Slip stitch in every chain across. Run tie through neckline holes of every one of these items. Sew a pom-pom to each end of tie.

SQUARES SHAWL

Each square measures 4½″ square. Make 55 squares, 11 triangles. Sew together as in diagram. Work single crochet edging all around. Fringe 2 sides of shawl.

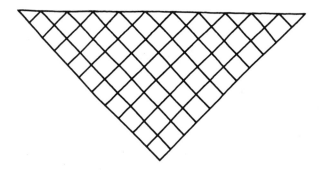

HEXAGONS SHAWL

Each hexagon measures 4½ inches across as shown. Make 63 hexagons. Sew together as in diagram. Fringe 2 sides of shawl.

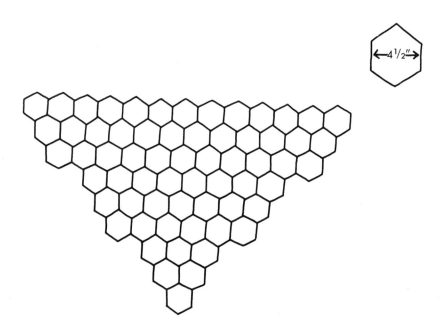

Glossary

Foreign Dictionary of Crochet Terms

ENGLISH	BRITISH	ITALIAN
crochet hook	crochet hook	uncinetto
chain	chain	catenella
stitch	stitch	maglia or punto
slip stitch	single crochet	punto scorso or mezza maglia bassa
single crochet	double crochet	maglia bassa
double crochet	treble crochet	maglia alta
triple crochet	double-treble crochet	maglia alta doppio
loop	loop	asola
yarn over	yarn over	fare un gettato
skip	skip	saltare
repeat from *	repeat from *	repetere da *

SPANISH	GERMAN	FRENCH
aguja de crochet	Hakelnadel	aiguille de crochet
cadena	kettenstich or Luftmasche	maille chainette
punto	Stich or Masche	maille
punto deslizado	Masche uberziehen	maille glissee
macizo doble	feste Masche	demi-bride
macizo triple	Stabchen	bride
macizo cuadruple	Doppelstabchen	double-bride
habilla	Schlinge	boucle
hilo por encima	1 Umschlag	faire un jete
saltar	auslassen	sauter
repetir desde*	wiederhole von *	reprendre a *

175

Yarn and Crochet Hook Compatibility Chart

	TYPE OF HOOK	SIZE OF HOOK
CROCHET COTTON	steel	00 0 1 2 3 4 5 6
COTTON STRING	aluminum	G H I
FINGERING / BABY YARN	aluminum	C D E
SPORT YARN	aluminum	E F G
RUG YARN or BULKY YARN	aluminum	J K Q
MOHAIR YARN	plastic or wood aluminum	G H I J
METALLIC YARN	aluminum	E F G H
MULTI-COLORED / OMBRE YARN	aluminum	E F G H I
RATTAIL	aluminum	I J K

	TYPE OF HOOK	*SIZE OF HOOK*
JUTE	aluminum	J
		K
RAFFIA / SYNTHETIC STRAW	aluminum	G
		H
		I
CREPE YARN	aluminum	E
		F
		G
FABRIC STRIPS	aluminum	J
		K
	plastic or wood	Q
WORSTED WEIGHT YARN (4 ply)	aluminum	G
		H
		I
		J

Patchwork Crochet Pattern Guide

Use the chart as a guide in pattern planning. Refer to pages 154, 155, and 156 for suggestions for organizing color patterns and joining.

179

Gauge Guidelines

Use the grid to measure for correct gauge. Each square of the grid equals ¼ inch.

   *If gauge is indicated for a project, such as Patchwork Crochet Fashions (page 160), check gauge with the grid by placing the crochet motif on the grid.

   *If gauge is not indicated for projects, such as afghans, shawls, and tote bags, all motifs for that project should be crocheted to the same size so joining will be smooth and easy. Check gauge of each motif by placing it on the grid.

   (Refer to page 17 for an explanation of gauge.)

Index